Growth Counseling for Mid-Years Couples

Creative Pastoral Care and Counseling Series
    Editor: Howard J. Clinebell, Jr.
    Associate Editor: Howard W. Stone

Growth Counseling for Mid-Years Couples

Howard J. Clinebell, Jr.

Fortress Press Philadelphia

We know that men and women need not fall into a stupor of mind and spirit by the time they are middle-aged. They need not relinquish as early as they do the resilience of youth and the capacity to learn and grow.*

—John W. Gardner

It is my conviction that what is called for now is "liberated marriage," a relationship in which two people who *like* each other, who *love* each other, and who are able to have fun together, and share the transcendent moments of life together, make a conscious commitment to each other's and their own growth.†

—Charlotte H. Clinebell

Library of Congress Catalog Card Number 76-007863

ISBN 0-8006-0558-6

5769F76   Printed in U.S.A.   1-558

Contents

Series Foreword

Let me share with you some of the hopes that are in the minds of those of us who helped to develop this series—hopes that relate directly to you as the reader. It is our desire and expectation that these books will be of help to you in developing better working tools as a minister-counselor. We hope that they will do this by encouraging your own creativity in developing more effective methods and programs for helping people live life more fully. It is our intention in this series to affirm the many things you have going for you as a minister in helping troubled persons—the many assets and resources from your religious heritage, your role as the leader of a congregation, and your unique relationship to individuals and families throughout the life cycle. We hope to help you reaffirm the *power of the pastoral* by the use of fresh models and methods in your ministry.

The aim of the series is not to be comprehensive with respect to topics but rather to bring innovative approaches to some major types of counseling. Although the books are practice-oriented, they also provide a solid foundation of theological and psychological insights. They are written primarily for ministers (and those preparing for the ministry), but we hope that they will also prove useful to other counselors who are interested in the crucial role of spiritual and value issues in all helping relationships. In addition we hope that the series will be useful in seminary courses, clergy support groups, continuing education workshops, and lay befriender training.

This is a period of rich new developments in counseling and psychotherapy. The time is ripe for a flowering of creative methods and insights in pastoral care and counseling.

Our expectation is that this series will stimulate grass-roots creativity as innovative methods and programs come alive for you. Some of the major thrusts that will be discussed in this series include a new awareness of the unique contributions of the theologically trained counselor, the liberating power of the human potentials orientation, an appreciation of the pastoral care function of the ministering congregation, the importance of humanizing systems and institutions as well as close relationships, the importance of pastoral *care* (and not just counseling), the many opportunities for caring ministries throughout the life cycle, the deep changes in male-female relationships, and the new psychotherapies such as Gestalt therapy, Transactional Analysis, educative counseling, and crisis methods. Our hope is that this series will enhance your resources for your ministry to persons by opening doorways to understanding of these creative thrusts in pastoral care and counseling.

In this volume, Howard J. Clinebell, Jr. has given us a practical guide to pastoral care and counseling of couples in their middle years. The book builds on his first book in this series, *Growth Counseling for Marriage Enrichment: Pre-Marriage and the Early Years.* He continues to develop his theme that marriage counseling does not need to be oriented only to pathology and problems but can be positive in focus, aiming at enrichment and growth. *Growth Counseling for Mid-Years Couples* has something to say about marriages which are already more than a few years old. It is about how you can continue (or start anew) to enhance the marriage relationship even when the children are grown and gone and you think you know all there is to know about your spouse.

One of the striking things about the book is how personal it is. Howard Clinebell writes not just as a clinical therapist observing middle-years marriages, but also as one who is experiencing these years of marriage himself: "This book reflects my own struggles and satisfactions in the mid-years." The book is also highly readable—clear, articulate, and practical. It is not a book to be read and then laid aside; you can apply it to your own marriage as well as to the marriages you encounter in your parish. It is useful as a monograph on marriage counseling but also as a resource guide for marriage enrichment groups within your parish. It is a book that mid-years couples themselves can enjoy and appreciate.

Many of you reading this book have already read one or more of Howard Clinebell's previous books and are aware of his impressive background. He is one of the most effective pastoral counselors and teachers of pastoral counseling and marriage enrichment in the United States. He has been a professor of pastoral counseling at the School of Theology at Claremont, California, for eighteen years, has traveled throughout the world lecturing and conducting workshops, and is the author of numerous books in his field.

I hope you enjoy the book as much as I have; I am confident that it will contribute much to your professional as well as your personal growth.

HOWARD W. STONE

How to Get the Most From This Book

Here are some suggestions for deriving maximum benefit from this book:

1) Read, discuss, and experience the book with your spouse or, if you're single, with a close friend.

2) Take time from your busy life to experience the growth tools and exercises. These methods will come alive for you and be more useful in your work if you first use them to enrich your own close relationships.

3) Review the principles and methods of growth counseling and marriage enrichment in the companion volume— *Growth Counseling for Marriage Enrichment: Pre-Marriage and the Early Years.* These principles and methods, which will not be repeated in this book, are also described in the cassette course, *Growth Counseling,* Part I, Course 1A. (See the Annotated Bibliography at the end of this book for the full references on all resources mentioned.)

4) As you use the book, jot down your ideas, questions, reactions, and plans in a small notebook. This notebook will become a growth journal, a log of your encounter with the ideas and methods of this book. Such a personal log can help you note the things worth remembering, as well as keep track of your ideas, growth experiences, and plans for implementing the methods which are relevant to your situation.

5) If the book proves to be helpful to you, try using it as an experiential learning resource with mid-years couples in a group or class. For example, invite three, four, or five couples who want to make good marriages better to join you and your spouse in using the book as a do-it-yourselves guide. Or,

use the book to improve the mid-years program in your church, school, or social agency.

This book is designed for two purposes—to provide resources and guidelines for ministers and other counselors for use in mid-years growth counseling and marriage enrichment; and to provide do-it-yourself help for mid-years couples who wish to enrich their own marriage. All the chapters except parts of 3 and 8 are directed to mid-years individuals and couples, as they might be addressed by a minister doing mid-years counseling or leading mid-years marriage enrichment events. Although the application of the book's ideas to the work of the pastor or other marriage enricher is self-evident, occasional explicit suggestions will be given to facilitate this application in the parish or other setting.

The book reflects my own struggles and satisfactions in the mid-years. It is a tentative statement and certainly not an exhaustive exploration of this life stage. My hope is that you will find it helpful in your contacts with persons in these years or in your own encounter with this rich, demanding stage of the life journey.

If you are in the mid-years, the book's basic message has two parts: (1) You have more going *for* you than you think you do—probably lots more! (2) Here are some tools for discovering and using the potential of the mid-years.

I am grateful to Scott Sullender for his help with this manuscript. And to Charlotte, who has helped make our mid-years such lively and eventful years, my heartfelt thanks.

HOWARD CLINEBELL

1. The Expanding Horizons of the Mid-Years

Men and women now in middle age can choose to make the next years matter. For this generation, a new time of life is possible . . . clearly compelling as it emerges sharp and crisp, from the mists of confusing change. No other generation has had the options it presents. . . . At this precise moment in time the pattern can be made . . . the new time of life generates an explorer's excitement.*

—Anne Simon

From a perspective halfway through the years from forty to sixty-five, I can say that the mid-years to date have been the most fulfilling and productive period of my life. They also have been a time of painful problems and accelerating losses. In our marriage these mid-years have brought the most satisfying companionship and the most stormy changes. The deeper companionship has been possible, in large part, because of the changes.

For most of the mid-years people I know, this period has brought new pressures and problems but also exciting new possibilities. As you may have discovered, the best way to cope constructively with the problems posed by this (or any) new life stage is to concentrate on developing the fresh potentials the new stage brings.

For many people, the mid-years are truly the "prime of life."† People in the mid-years are savoring life and contributing in satisfying ways to their families, their communities, their churches, and their jobs. For many couples, these are years which bring the rich fulfillment of time-tested relationship, rejuvenated intimacy, and lusty, reawakened sex.

* For this and all other notes in this book, see the Notes section beginning on p. 80.

But for many others, the rich possibilities of the mid-years are undiscovered and undeveloped. The good news is that insights and methods are now available by which such persons can renew their inner lives and enliven their marriages.

The new mid-years are a gift to humankind. The dramatic increase in life expectancy in this century in the so-called developed countries has created a new life stage for the majority of people there. Never before have so many human beings lived long enough or been healthy enough to enjoy a rich, active life through the mid-years and beyond. Our times offer unprecedented resources and opportunities for using these new years well. The horizons of the mid-years are expanding. The pages that follow offer guidelines for responding to the challenge of these new years, suggestions for making your mid-years one of the most fulfilling periods of your life.

Understanding the Mid-Years

To enrich mid-years marriages it is important to understand the nature and dynamics of this life period. The years between forty and sixty-five actually include two distinct life stages. Mid-years I, roughly the first half of these years, is the time when adolescents are still in the home. Mid-years II, the pre-retirement, empty nest period, confronts a couple with different problems, needs, and possibilities. Families with more than one child have a transition stage between mid-years I and II, as young adults exit, one by one, from their parental home.

The changes and losses which accompany the movement from one life stage to another force us to learn new ways to satisfy our basic needs for self-esteem, meaning, identity, and nurturing relationships. The process of letting go of one stage and learning ways of satisfying basic heart hungers in a new stage normally brings feelings of grief, pressure, and anxiety.

For some persons the entrance into mid-years I and mid-years II produces obvious crises with acute anxiety and floundering behavior. For those at the other extreme, the transition is relatively smooth. They do not experience a "mid-years crisis." But for many between these extremes, the movement into mid-years I and mid-years II produces a quiet crisis which is painful though not devastating.

Let us look at one mid-years couple, the Morgans (not their real name), to get inside their experience:

Karen and Roger Morgan, forty-seven and forty-eight respectively, have been married for twenty-six years. Their daughter Judy, twenty-two, has been away at college for three years. Recently she informed her parents, to their great relief, of her plans to marry the young man with whom she has been living. Peter, nineteen, is attending the local community college and is the "achiever" among the children. Robert, seventeen, is a junior in high school. His poor marks, rejection of religion, and dabbling in drugs cause feelings of failure and anger in his parents.

Roger is preoccupied with the heavy pressures of his job in middle management in a large company. He feels he has "plateaued out." Often he works evenings and weekends to "catch up" and to try to stay ahead of several bright younger associates whom he fears will be promoted over him. The increasing financial stresses of inflation, college expenses, and nursing home care for his aging mother, put a chronic load on Roger's mind. He is drinking more, especially on weekends, to deaden the dull ache of feeling trapped on the job treadmill.

Karen, like many middle-class wives, is experiencing the mid-years in ways that are very different from her husband. Her life and satisfactions have been centered in children and home. The emptying nest confronts her with the threat, as she put it in a moment of self-awareness, of soon being "half unemployed." The beginning of her menopause brings mixed feelings of relief from the worry about unwanted pregnancy together with the grief of lost youth and vitality. She is still feeling the painful loss of her father who died two years ago. As she thinks about the future, her options seem limited and bleak. She has toyed with the possibility of looking for a part-time job outside the home. But she knows that her B.A. in liberal arts and her lack of job experience would limit severely her employment options, even if it were not for Roger's resistance to her working outside the home.

Roger and Karen have had a conventional "good marriage" through the years. But his preoccupation with his job and her preoccupation with the children have left little time for their relationship. Except for worried conversations about their children, there has been little communicating on the level of either person's real pain or hopes. Sex was good in the early years but of late it has become increasingly infrequent, hurried, and less satisfying, especially for Karen. Their marriage has become dull. It lacks the moments of playfulness and joy which it had during the first ten years. Karen and Roger feel caught in a four-way squeeze—between the demands of their still-dependent children and of their aging parents, and the pressures of Roger's job and Karen's awareness of a future devoid of challenge.

Both Karen and Roger are aware of the gulf that's growing between them. Both sense that there is much more to life and to marriage than they are finding. Because she is more dependent on their relationship, and lacks the satisfactions Roger gets from his job, Karen feels the marital vacuum more acutely. As she put it during one of their frequent, futile arguments, "At times I feel like we're living alone in the same house—like you care more about your damn job than about me or our marriage!"

Both Roger and Karen want to stay married to each other. Behind their loneliness, hurt, and anger, there is still a mutual caring. Yet they are feeling painfully unfulfilled in their relationship. Unless they can deepen their communication, their creeping alienation probably will worsen as their nest empties.

Karen and Roger are each experiencing a personal mid-years crisis. Both feel the grief of their losses and the pressure of a contracting future. Both are in a personal crisis of identity, self-esteem, and meaning. Each person's inner crisis is enhanced by the other's pain and by the crisis in their relationship. Thus they are caught in a negative cycle of mutual distress. For them to interrupt this cycle will require personal renewal for each and the revitalization of their marriage.

It was the pain of their mid-years crisis that brought the Morgans to a weekend marriage enrichment retreat sponsored by their church. Roger came reluctantly, pressured by Karen. Both came with uneasiness about what would happen, but also with a faint hope that it somehow might help lessen the pain and restore some of the sparkle in their marriage.

At the enrichment retreat, the Morgans were encouraged, during a communication session, to tell each other what things caused them grief and pain, and what caused feelings of joy and esteem. In this session they discovered, to their surprise, that they had many of the same feelings of anger, anxiety, guilt, and grief. They also became aware of positive feelings. In spite of their problems, both agreed that in some ways "we've never had it so good." They agreed that they have fewer money worries and more security than ever before. They realized that both are in generally good health. In spite of their problems and emotional distance, they realized that they still value their marriage. They have been through a lot of ups and downs together, and they have come to value much in their life together. They realize that they could now have more time together than they have had at any time since their courting days. The awareness of these assets—both actual and potential—awakened hope for further positive change.

At the retreat they decided to set aside time each day to communicate. During these times, they talk about their inner feelings and about the practical decisions they can make to help reduce the pressure of Roger's job and allow Karen to use her energies and abilities as the children leave. Discovering as the weeks passed that they still *can* communicate, and at a more satisfying level, about what really matters to them, is the greatest hope-awakener of all. After one such discussion Karen decided, with Roger's concurrence, to enroll in a nearby university for a master's degree in accounting. This is a field to which she had always been attracted. The degree will open the door to work outside the home if she chooses. Together, with the encouragement of their support group of four other couples (which grew out of the retreat), the Morgans are creating a new future for themselves and their marriage. They are discovering the exciting possibilities which the mid-years can hold for them.

Three Keys to Mid-Years Creativity

Personal and marital renewal in the mid-years depend on implementing three working principles in one's individual life and in one's relationships: growth, intentionality, and generativity. As the Morgans are beginning to discover, these are the keys to a more creative mid-years lifestyle.

Growth

To handle the mid-years constructively requires continuing growth, i.e., potentializing. A recent psychological study concluded: "The evolution of a personality continues through the fifth decade of life. A person does not possess the full range of his uniqueness after merely passing through adolescence. . . . The process of formation continues."* Potentializing, on an individual level, means the actualization of more and more of one's unused strengths, including the unique assets of one's particular life stage. A potentializing marriage is one in which each person simultaneously is growing and encouraging the other to grow.

Intentionality

This means choosing goals for one's life, choosing goals together for the marriage, and then working toward them. Intentionality involves claiming and using one's power to create a better future, rather than merely drifting or blaming circumstances and each other. A perceptive student of the mid-years declares: "The essence of whether one experiences 'a Renaissance or the Dark Ages' in middle life seems to me to depend a great deal on the degree to which one can use

change effectively rather than deny its existence."* Intentionality means becoming more the pilot and less the prisoner
of the inevitable changes mid-life brings. This attitude liber-
ates persons to reach out actively from their own inner centers, to choose and act on the best of their options, however
limited or abundant these may be.

A friend of mine who has a demanding and often frustrating job, has a poster on her wall which reads: "If life gives you
a lemon, make lemonade!" By the middle years, most of us
have a sizable collection of lemons. Some of these can be
turned into positive resources. Intentionality frees one to use
the precious time that is left in one's life, however long or
limited that may be. Intentionality allows one to choose one's
attitudes toward the unchangeable and tragic in one's life.
Responding actively to both the tragic and the joyful aspects
of life frees one from drifting and permits one to swim in the
direction one chooses, in spite of the turbulence and the cur-
rent. In a phrase from Gestalt therapy, it lets one "take back
one's power!"

Generativity

A third key to mid-years creativity involves self-fulfillment
through self-investment, or, to paraphrase a biblical insight,
finding one's life by investing it in others. Erik Erikson (who
coined the term generativity) sees the development of generativity as the central life task and challenge in these years:
"In this stage, a man and a woman must have defined for
themselves what and whom they come to care for, what they
can do well, and how they plan to take care of what they have
started and created."† Generativity involves generating and
nurturing life by caring for children (one's own or others),
the earth, people-serving institutions, culture, art, or those in
need. In short, it means caring about and for the future, by
investing something of yourself in nurturing those persons,
causes, and values which will live after you and will help in
some small way to make the planet a better place for the

children of the human family. For us who are in the mid-years, the alternatives are clear—generate or stagnate. The truth, I suppose, is that most of us do some of both.

A Unified Creative Lifestyle

These three working concepts are simply different facets of a unified creative lifestyle in the mid-years. The path to personal renewal and marriage enrichment is the same path. It consists of becoming more growing, intentional, and generative persons. Translating these principles into one's daily life and relationship opens up the future. The pages that follow will suggest methods of doing this.

The pain resulting from unlived life and wasted potential becomes more and more oppressive during the mid-years. Three common ways of deadening this pain are frantic activity (work addiction), excessive drinking and pill popping, and desperate "last fling" sexual affairs. These escapes usually prove to be pseudosolutions. They take the edge off harsh reality temporarily, but in the long run make one's reality even harsher. The prevention or healing of these person-hurting escapes from mid-years pain involves becoming more growing, intentional, and generative persons, and thus discovering the zest and the lift which the Gospel of John calls "life in all its fullness" (John 10:10, NEB).

The Importance of Mid-Years Programs

At the present time, over one-fifth of all Americans are between the ages of forty and sixty-five. Many of these people have significant social influence as well as personal resources and potential. They hold the handles of power in most institutions. The wholeness of their lives and relationships have an enormous influence on the welfare of society. Enrichment of their lives and marriages will benefit themselves, their adolescent children, and all the social institutions, including the churches, in which they have a prominent part.

By the year 2000, it is estimated that the population's center of gravity will have shifted from youth to the early mid-years. The number of adults between thirty-five and forty-nine will have increased by seventy-five percent, and those between fifty and sixty-four, by twenty-seven percent (in contrast to only five percent increase among children and youth).*

This emerging new mid-years majority challenges all our people-serving institutions to develop more imaginative, effective programs of enrichment and education to help mid-years adults use more of their assets and potentialities. Churches have an unrivaled opportunity in this area, because so many mid-years persons are and will be among their members. To be lifelong human development centers churches must develop more innovative, dynamic approaches that can meet the unique growth needs of mid-years individuals and couples.

The greatest danger of the so-called dangerous years is that so many will not experience the flowering of potential that is possible in this mid-life period. Innovative life enrichment and marriage renewal programs in our churches, schools, and social agencies can help mid-years persons confront the challenge and the choices, the pain and the possibilities, and from this confrontation begins the adventure of new growth. Mid-years persons and couples can discover and exercise a new usefulness to the community, not possible before these years.

2. Twelve Strategies for Making the Most of the Mid-Years

This is the wonder of the crisis of middle age; its challenges
are the greatest opportunity one has ever had to become more
truly alive and oneself.*
—Edna J. LeShan

The mid-years offer opportunities for a fresh flowering of
one's life and one's intimate relationships. There are certain
strategies which have proved to be helpful in developing these
possibilities.

Listing the Strategies

Twelve such strategies are mentioned here as practical methods for renewing one's inner wellsprings and helping a marriage become a more fulfilling bond of mutual growth. I will
list them as I might in a growth counseling session or a marriage enrichment group. I believe you'll find them useful both
for do-it-yourself enrichment and for helping others maximize
these years. Those strategies which are explored in later
chapters, will be mentioned only briefly in this overview.

Strategy 1. Identify the Real Assets and New Possibilities of the Mid-Years.

Personally, I find it easier to be aware of my liabilities and
problems than of my assets and strengths. But focusing on
assets and strengths helps to awaken hopes and motivation for
continuing growth in any of us. Such a positive focus also
provides the best context for coping constructively with the
real losses and liabilities of these years.

In your growth log or journal list all the strengths, assets,
and new possibilities you can think of in your present life

stage.   List everything that is or could be a positive resource.
Don't forget such basic assets as your accrued experience and
the fragments of wisdom you have acquired through the years,
or the fact that you are probably not as old, physically or
psychologically, as were people your age a generation ago.*/
[A solidus (/) means put the book aside while you complete
the task.]   On another page of your growth log, list all the
assets, strengths and potentialities of your spouse as you see
him or her./   On another page, list the assets, strengths, and
new possibilities which you see in your marriage./

Now, share your three lists with your spouse./   If you are
in a couples enrichment group, give each other the "gift" of
stating what each of you sees as the strengths of the other
individual and of your marriage./   In your growth log, add
the assets of which you have become aware as a result of the
affirmation of your spouse (and perhaps your group)./

Now, having looked at the positive side of the mid-years,
list the losses, problems, and liabilities of your life stage./
Compare your list with that of your spouse and discuss how
you feel about your liabilities when seen in the context of your
assets./

**Strategy 2. Use Your Assets Intentionally by Choosing to Do Those
Things That Will Help Create a Better Future for Yourself and Your
Marriage.**

The purpose of this exercise is to respond to your live options intentionally, using more of the strengths and assets you
have identified.   In your growth journal, list all the things you
really would like to do in order to use your assets to make
your life and your marriage more fulfilling./   Now choose two
of these goals and write out a plan for moving toward them,
including a timetable for doing so.   Be concrete and specific
in your planning./

Now share your list of goals and your action plans with
your spouse.   Invite your spouse (and perhaps your sharing
group) to add things they would like for you to do to use more
of your potentialities.   Give each other feedback in this way./

Now, with your spouse, develop a joint action plan for improving your marriage, drawing on the assets each of you has identified./

I hope that these experiences of reflection and sharing have made you more aware of having an open future with a variety of challenges and options. Choosing specific goals and implementing plans for achieving them increases the intentionality in your lives and in your marriage. Such active intentionality may not be easy at first, particularly if it is a new way of functioning. But, as you practice and master this approach to the mid-years, it can open the door to a better future.

Strategy 3. Befriend and Enrich Your "Inner Companion."

In the mid-years it is important to take time to become better friends with the only person you are really with from birth to death. See to it that "when one *is* alone one still has a very good companion—oneself."* It is easy to become so rushed and outer-directed in the mid-years that one's inner friend is treated as a stranger, if not an enemy. When this happens, all of one's close relationships suffer. To have a mutually-enlivening relationship, a couple needs to be in touch and in tune with themselves as individuals.

So, slow down and get reacquainted with yourself. Cherish closeness with your spouse, but don't try to make even that precious relationship a substitute for developing your inner life. Inner enrichment and relationship enrichment are two essential and complementary sides of the same coin.

Befriending yourself begins with accepting who and where you are. This is the starting point of all personal growth. Inner enrichment probably involves expanding your consciousness and your intellectual horizons. It includes nourishing and enjoying your spiritual life.

For many of us, the mid-years precipitate a crisis in our spiritual life. Creative coping with this spiritual crisis requires enlivening one's functional faith, increasing one's moments of transcendence, renewing the sense of meaning in one's life, and increasing the awareness of one's loving connectedness with the Spirit of the universe. Spiritual enrichment in a marriage relationship involves increased *sharing* of a couple's meanings, working faith, and moments of transcendence.

Strategy 4. Update Your Values and Priorities.

The mid-years confront many of us with the need to reexamine our priorities and values, and to do a mid-course correction of these inner guidelines. Am I investing my limited time, energy, and resources in the things that matter most to me and to the world I will someday leave to our children? I find that some things I gave a great deal of myself to in the earlier years—acquiring things and getting ahead—no longer satisfy deeply. The revising of skewed priorities is essential to a more fulfilling lifestyle.

Joint value clarification, as a couple, often is valuable in these years. Can we affirm and even learn to enjoy the differences as well as the similarities in our values?

Strategy 5. Enrich and Strengthen Your Community of Caring—Your Network of Nurturing Relationships.

The mid-years are a time when poverty in one's relationships becomes increasingly costly. Every person needs several persons with whom he or she can experience acceptance, love, and caring. Many of us are surfeited by superficial contacts with many people, but impoverished by a lack of depth relationships.

In strengthening one's marriage, it is important not to neglect investing oneself in the supportive circle of friends and/or relatives who make up one's extended family. This wider circle of caring people gives stability and strength to a marriage, particularly during crises. The heavy time pressures of the mid-years make it easy to neglect the mutual nurture which alone keeps relationships healthy and growing.

Continuing nurture of your caring community allows you to enjoy it more. Communicating regularly with those who matter to you can bring satisfying rewards. For example, a simple thing such as taking ten minutes each day to write a note of sincere affirmation and appreciation to some friend, relative, or colleague can nourish them, enrich your relationship, and bring remarkably satisfying feedback.

Strategy 6. Rethink Your Vocational and Avocational Lives Together (in Light of Your Revised Priorities) and Do What Is Necessary to Make Each of These More Challenging and Fulfilling.

At an enrichment workshop one mid-years engineer declared during a session on life-investment planning, "I'm in work I no longer find challenging—trapped by economic necessity and by career decisions I made twenty-five years ago when I was a mere kid." He eventually decided that, although a career change was not feasible, he *could* develop a much more fulfilling avocational life—for example, by pursuing a long-latent interest in learning to throw pots.

Mid-life career changes are increasingly common and accepted in our society for both women and men. For women whose career has been raising children it is essential that they develop realistic plans which will allow them to use their energies and talents in satisfying ways as the children leave. Such plans often involve new careers for pay or, in other cases, pursuing fulfilling volunteer and avocational interests.

In our case Charlotte's mid-course career change involved her return to graduate school to receive training as a psychotherapist. Her moving into a second career changed the dynamics of our relationship. These changes threatened me for a time but proved to be the beginning of a new phase in our marriage with more equality, sharing, and companionship. Having a career of her own for pay has helped Charlotte develop a new and more positive identity as an autonomous person. Becoming a two-career couple brought new pressures and problems, but also new possibilities in our marriage. Couples who share both child rearing and outside-the-home work more equally than we did probably have a less radical adjustment when the mid-years come. There is much to commend this equalitarian approach to marriage, as many younger couples are discovering.

Strategy 7. Discover and Commit Yourself to a Cause That Excites You.

Find your challenge and then give yourself to it with enthusiasm. A compelling life investment becomes more and more important after the age of forty, because it gives life purpose and zest. Such a dynamic commitment is the very center of generative lifestyle, enabling you to invest yourself in those persons, institutions, and causes whose constructive influence will live on after you have made your final exit. This kind of self-investment is an essential, deeply satisfying element in personal renewal.

It helps enliven mid-years marriages for couples to find an exciting shared challenge which is much bigger than their relationship. We know a mid-years couple who are pouring themselves with passionate enthusiasm into working to help solve the interrelated problems of world hunger, overpopulation, and environmental pollution. By working through organizations which are dedicated to finding creative solutions to these problems they are making a small but significant contribution to a more growth-producing world. They are discovering enrichment and enjoyment in working together as volunteers for causes that excite them both.

In the mid-years, each of us needs to find satisfying answers to this basic question: "What am I doing to help make my community a better place because of my having lived here?"

Strategy 8. Let Go of Your Energy-Wasting Load of Anger, Guilt, and Grief.

By mid-life everyone has experienced an abundance of mistakes, failures, missed opportunities, and disappointments. Much mid-years depression results from a deadening load of these accumulated feelings. Personal creativity and the ability to live zestfully in the here-and-now are diminished by this energy-wasting burden. Unresolved guilt, remorse, anger, and grief form a vicious cycle of intertwined, mutually reinforcing pain. Learning how to gain release regularly from this load is difficult but essential to creative mid-years living.

Much of the anger experienced in the mid-years is a natural response to the losses of these years. A youth-valuing culture tends to reduce self-esteem and increases anger in most people as they grow older. Anger turned inward on oneself produces depression. Chronic, low level depression causes or complicates many mid-years marriage problems, including problems of sexual nonresponsiveness.

Since the mid-years usually bring accelerating losses, grief is a large component in the crisis. This makes it crucial to learn to do one's "grief work"—the work of experiencing the pain and talking out the feeling with an understanding, accepting person, so that the wounds in one's spirit can heal fully. Unresolved guilt and resentment frequently infects the grief wounds, preventing them from healing.

While I was revising this manuscript, my father died. Although he was eighty-six and had had a good life, I was confronted with powerful feelings of loss, remorse, and anger that I could not have anticipated. For the first time I understood in my heart the words of a friend spoken four years earlier when her mother died: "Somehow I feel I am next in line!" The death of parents makes the awareness of one's own eventual death unavoidable. Studies using the Rorschach inkblot test have revealed that subconscious preoccupation with death is very common among those over fifty.*

Guilt and remorse are very prevalent creativity-robbers in the mid-years. As Nena and George O'Neill observe: "You can't change the past . . . but you *can* change the future. To spend time and energy lamenting the past is to waste the present and the future."† In the mid-years, the present and future become increasingly precious. It behooves us to move from the alienation of guilt to the reconciliation of forgiveness.

Here are some practical steps for letting go of the excess baggage of accumulated negative feelings:

First, face your feelings and bring them out into the light of a trust-full relationship. To ignore painful feelings is to leave them festering in the cellar of your psyche. It may help you to face and resolve your feelings if you do a systemic inventory, using your growth log. Begin by listing all the burdensome feelings of which you become aware when you take time to go inside yourself. List the hurts, resentments, guilt feelings, and griefs that weigh on your mind. Do this with your spouse or a trusted friend present for support. If you have buried your feelings for a long time, it may be difficult or impossible to become aware of them now. But if depression or ineffectiveness in living makes you suspect that burdensome feelings are there, by all means have some sessions with a well-trained pastoral counselor or psychotherapist to help you surface and resolve the feelings.

Second, take several sessions to talk out your painful feelings with your partner. Let the feelings flow. Expressing them openly in a relationship of trust usually helps reduce the burden of such feelings. If talking alone does not lighten the load, try expressing your feelings in nondestructive physical ways. For example, I find that striking a bed violently and repeatedly with my fist, while I yell unrestrainedly, helps drain off pent-up anger and lift depression.

It often strengthens a marriage to share the things that give each partner pain. However, it is important not to confess things that may damage the relationship. If such things are burdening your mind, get the help of a trained counselor. If talking together about your feelings does not improve things, or even makes them worse, it is essential to seek professional help. A series of sessions with a skilled counselor can be one of the best investments in the future that you will ever make. The goal is the fullest possible liberation of your energies and your creativity.

Third, do whatever you must to make amends, repair damaged relationships, and release your emotional load. Taking reparative action is an essential step in the unburdening process. But before you take action, check out your plan with your spouse, or some other objective person, to make sure it is constructive.

Fourth, in those things which you cannot change, restore,

or improve try to make peace with the past. Accept yourself as having done all that you can and then accept God's forgiveness. Affirm the present and the future by investing yourself in constructive living now.

Guilt, disappointment, and resentment accumulate within a close relationship, as they do within an individual. By mid-marriage such feelings often have built up like a wall between the partners, diminishing or shutting off satisfying communication. As a couple lowers this wall, loving, tender feelings usually flow spontaneously between them.

Strategy 9. Let Yourself Really Live in the Now.

List in your growth log the things that make you feel most alive (in contrast to merely existing)./ What are the things that you have always wanted to do but never taken the time? Now list these dreams in your growth log./

As marriage partners, share your lists with each other./ Plan ways of increasing the "alive" times in your individual lives and in your marriage./

Now plan ways of helping each other turn more of your individual and shared dreams into reality. For example, if you have always wanted to write poetry, sit down in a quiet place and begin right now. Or, if you both have dreamed of acquiring a waterbed, devise a way to do this within the next month./ Do not put off the satisfaction of living fully in the now. Lots of mid-life people are realizing long-postponed dreams. They are "turning on" to life by developing creative and satisfying interests.

Strategy 10. Increase the Variety and Frequency of Your Play, Including Playful Sex.

I find that life gets to be a drag unless I experience regularly the renewal of pleasuring. As a workaholic, I tend to short-change myself and our marriage in this vital area. Reserving regular pleasure-and-play (P and P) times in our datebooks helps protect these times from the pressure of overcrowded schedules. You're lucky, of course, if your lifestyle gives you adequate play spontaneously, without planning ahead.

Recreation and the satisfying playful aspects of work help to recharge the inner batteries that give lift to your life and your marriage. So, raise the pleasure quotient of your lives by enjoying a warm whirlpool bath, a show, an evening on the town, a stroll along the lake, a relaxing book, an uplifting worship experience, a leisurely roll in the hay—whatever you both find pleasurable. Take turns choosing what you will do during these pleasuring times. Surprise each other. In the language of Transactional Analysis, let your "Child" sides romp together.* Enjoy yourself, it's earlier than you think!

Strategy 11. Treat Your Minuses as Potential Pluses.

The fact that tragedy, pain, and loss are part of the fabric from which our lives are woven becomes increasingly inescapable in the mid-years. Nearly everyone's life has a tragic, messy side. After the worst of a crisis has passed, it may be possible to see redeeming aspects in the experience. Through this awareness, a total minus can be transformed into at least a partial plus.

Can you recall a traumatic crisis that actually brought you closer to each other? If so, discuss why it did so./ Painful experiences, much as we dislike them, can strengthen our spiritual muscles for coping with future crises. Our pain can enable us to reach out with more empathy and help to others going through similar dark valleys.

Early in my mid-years I developed diabetes. This was a severe shock to my grandiose self-image. It was and is a frustrating nuisance to which I sometimes still respond with anger. But as I have made partial peace with the reality of my handicap, unexpected fringe benefits have emerged. My experience has strengthened the empathetic bond I feel with others who have handicaps and with persons who have gone through any kind of major loss. Life feels much more like a precious gift than it did before. When I stop to reflect on this, I am aware that my life *is* literally a gift—a gift from the two Canadian physicians who discovered insulin. It is a gift that I accept and affirm to the extent that I live life as fully, joyfully, and productively as I can.

Strategy 12. Be Kind to Your Body; Give It Care and Respect.

Mid-years stress and fatigue diminish unnecessarily the full enjoyment of these good years for many of us. To make the most of all dimensions of mid-life, cut down your calories and get adequate rest and regular exercise to keep your body in good tone. Your self-esteem probably will rise, your mental acuity increase, and your sex life get sexier if your physical organism is treated with care. The aim is simply to do the commonsense things which will allow you to enjoy and use your body efficiently—rather than letting your body use you. I find, for example, that if I allow myself to get so rushed that I neglect adequate rest or jogging, my mind gets sluggish and I "spin my wheels" when I try to do creative things.

Implementing the Strategies

I hope that these twelve suggested strategies have stimulated you to think of other ways to make the most of your mid-years. Jot down these ideas now in your growth journal. /

Now, let your mind reflect on all the strategies, including the ones you may have added. Which ones raise your energy level? Which seem most important in your life and your marriage? / Discuss your response with your spouse, and devise plans for implementing the strategies which you decide will help you make the mid-years fulfilling for you and your marriage.

If you work in church or community with mid-years persons, reflect on how you can use these twelve strategies in this work. Decide on ways to incorporate them in your mid-years counseling and enrichment programs. /

3. Enriching Mid-Years Marriages

In self-actualizing people the quality of love satisfactions and sex satisfactions both improve with the age of the relationship.*

—Abraham Maslow

Three factors in our society make marriage enrichment in the mid-years vitally important. The first is increased longevity. Creative monogomy can continue for most couples only if they have learned to update their covenant and revitalize their relationship at each changing life stage. By the mid-years marriage covenants that have not been revised are obsolete and unfulfilling in some important aspects.

The rising consciousness and expectations of women is the second factor which makes mid-marriage enrichment so important. Profound changes are occurring in women-men relationships, shaking the very foundation of more and more traditional marriages. Many mid-years couples have built their marriages through the years on traditional, one-up/one-down roles. Now, women increasingly are insisting on full equality. This often threatens their husbands, and conflict escalates between them. Marriage enrichment should be an instrument for liberating such marriages. It should encourage the couples to initiate the basic changes which will enable them to develop a more mutually fulfilling relationship. In an enrichment group couples can experience that blend of caring and confrontation which will help them move *through* their conflict to a better relationship built on an active commitment to each other's growth. Marriages can flourish fully only if there is such a commitment which produces equal opportunities for both parties to have fulfilling, productive lives.

The third factor making marriage enrichment crucial is the epidemic of loneliness in our urbanized, mobile society—a loneliness that becomes increasingly oppressive in the mid-years. A loving, growing marriage is one of the best places to have a trust-full, nonexploitative, depth relationship with another human being. Enriching a marriage can help it become a refreshing oasis of belonging. Each of us needs such an oasis to live constructively in our society.

The Values of Mid-Years Marriage Enrichment

A mid-course correction is valuable for any marriage. In a long-term relationship, as in a rocket flight, even a small change of direction at the midpoint can make a major difference in its moving toward the goal.* For couples with open communication self-enrichment can be effective, although the mutual encouragement of an enrichment group can make their efforts even more enjoyable and beneficial. Where communication is partially blocked, as in the case of the Morgans, a well-led group is essential. For mid-years couples in severe or chronic marriage crises, competent marriage counseling should precede involvement in enrichment events. After such counseling, marriage enrichment can help a couple continue the growth they began in counseling.

The "living happily ever after" myth is revealed as a patent fallacy in many mid-years marriages. Approximately one-fourth of the over one million couples who divorce each year in the United States have been married fifteen years or more. In the last five years, divorce among couples married twenty years or more has increased fifty percent.† Most studies of marriages show a gradual disenchantment and a declining degree of marital satisfactions, especially for women, through the child-rearing years. The emotional distancing which occurs during these years often becomes permanent unless outside help is sought.‡

Couples who are still friends and lovers after one or more decades of marriage are almost always those who have worked at strengthening and enriching their relationships. A recent survey revealed that many mid-marrieds *do* still care about each other and their marriage. To the statement, For me marriage has been a good thing, the percentage responding yes declined from age twenty-two to thirty-five; but then it rose gradually until at age fifty-one it was back to the level of age twenty-one respondents! To the question, How important are these people to you overall? the importance of "spouse" rose very gradually with each age category.*

If you are a mid-years couple who still love each other, but want to freshen up your marriage, marriage enrichment is for you. Statements like this appear frequently on the evaluation sheets of participants at the end of marriage enrichment events: "We haven't communicated like this in years. It feels great!" During one marriage enrichment session, I remarked (in discussing the impact of aging on marriage): "One morning you look across the breakfast table and suddenly it hits you—I'm married to a grandmother!" At this point a lively mid-years husband interrupted with a twinkle and a gleam in his eye: "Wow, what a grandmother!" Obviously that couple had learned how to maintain the sparkle in their marriage.

Goals of Mid-Years Marriage Enrichment

A good growing marriage in the mid-years is an achievement of which the two partners have a right to be proud. The goal of all marriage enrichment is to "make good marriages better" by helping couples develop more intimate, open relationships with full equality and positive fidelity.† In the mid-years, achieving this goal usually involves couples' revitalizing their relationships by increasing their mutual growth, their sense of intentionality, and their active generativity.

Mid-years marriage enrichment aims at both personal and marriage enrichment. It seeks to help couples practice *liberating love*—a caring whose central commitment is to liberating the full gifts of both persons. If I love you, I care passionately about what enables you to grow. Liberating love is also synergistic love. This is love that expands the personhood of each individual and makes the relationship more than the sum of what the two bring to it.

Here are some of the things which, as a mid-years couple,

you may need to do to revitalize your relationship: (a) Do a careful evaluation of where you are and where you want to go in your marriage. (b) Rethink your guiding values and priorities. (c) Develop a more equalitarian relationship with equal opportunities for both to grow. (d) Renegotiate a more mutually fulfilling marriage covenant. (e) Strengthen your companionship and your nurturing communication. (f) Learn better ways to resolve conflict and interrupt cycles of mutual hurting. (g) Enliven your sex life. (h) Increase your shared outreach. (i) Deepen your spiritual intimacy. (j) Develop better ways to cope collaboratively with teenage children. (k) Deal constructively with the problems of aging parents. (l) Discover the new pleasures and possibilities of the mid-years, including the empty nest.

If you lead marriage enrichment workshops, and do counseling, your approach should help couples accomplish these mid-years tasks.

Tools for Mid-Years Marriage Enrichment

The relationship-building tools for use in marriage enrichment are essentially the same as for any stage of marriage. The same is true of the various methods of setting up and leading marriage enrichment workshops, groups, and retreats. These methods are described in chapters 4 and 5 in my earlier volume in this series.* Here are some additional tools which are useful for couples at any stage, but particularly for mid-years couples. They are presented as they might be by a pastor in an enrichment group or growth counseling session.

A Marriage Checkup

A mid-course correction should begin by your doing a careful evaluation of the course of your marriage—where you have come together, where you are now, and where you want to go in the future. There are various ways of doing this.

Some couples prefer an unstructured approach in which they simply use four time-segments of approximately twenty minutes each:

Segment 1. Share and compare your thoughts about the

most important developments and achievements of your years together.

Segment 2. Share your thoughts about the strengths, assets, problems, and limitations of your present relationship.

Segment 3. Discuss the kind of marriage you would each like to have a year from now and, in the light of this, select concrete goals for your marriage.

Segment 4. Devise a workable plan for taking steps toward these shared goals. In an enrichment group or retreat each couple is then invited to "check out" their plan with a sharing group of three or four other couples.

A variation of this method involves the use of paper and crayons:

Segment 1. In your growth journal draw a sketch of your present relationship, including its strengths and its problems, using colors that best depict your feelings. Do it quickly. Don't plan it. Just let your fingers draw the first thing that comes to you./ When you have both finished, share your drawings with each other./

Segment 2. Now draw a picture of the relationship you would like to have a year from now./

Segment 3. Share and compare your pictures of your hopes and dreams for the future./ Working together, draw a single picture that incorporates both of your hopes./

Segment 4. Write a joint plan for doing the things that will help you move toward the marriage you both want.

Crayons and a large piece of paper are also needed for the marriage self-evaluation tool called "The Intentional Journey," which uses the symbolism of the marital journey: Each person draw two parallel lines across the paper longways at least 2½ inches apart to represent the road of your marital journey. Let the place where the road begins on the left represent the first time you met. The end of the road on the right represents the completion of your relationship at some point in the future./ Now, beginning at the left, draw a line across the road to mark your wedding, and other lines to represent the passage of each five years since then, including the future./ Using colors which symbolize your feelings, quickly draw a symbol or simple sketch depicting the most significant events or developments in each five-year section of your journey together./ In the future segments, draw what you hope will occur./ Share and compare your drawings; see what you can learn about each other./ Decide what changes you must make in your lives to move toward the goals you discovered you have in common./

Each of these exercises can facilitate deeper understanding of how each person remembers the past and what each hopes for in the future. The use of one of the above communication tools can enhance your awareness of the wealth of shared experiences in the past and your ability to mold the future of your marriage with an increasing degree of intentionality.

Some couples find that the "Marital Intimacy Checkup" and the "Marital Intimacy Action Plan" described in *The Intimate Marriage* provide helpful structure for a do-it-yourself checkup.* These simple instruments encourage reflection, dialogue, and action around twelve types of intimacy—sexual, emotional, intellectual, aesthetic, creative, recreational, work, crisis, conflict, commitment, spiritual, and communication intimacy. The use of these instruments encourages mid-years couples who feel "stuck in a rut" to explore and develop fresh dimensions of their relationship. If you prefer a more comprehensive marital checkup, *The Mirages of Marriage* by William Lederer and Don Jackson lists forty-five probing questions which focus on key issues in any marriage.†

The important thing is not the form your marriage inventory takes but that you take a careful look at the strengths and limitations of your present relationship and, in the light of this, do what is required to improve it in ways of your own choosing. It is crucial that each person's dissatisfactions and unmet needs be examined fully and that your plans for the future provide you both with equal opportunity for fulfilled lives.

Revising Your Covenant

In the process of evaluation just described the need for updating your marriage covenant or contract was implied. But since recontracting is such a crucial skill in both mid-years marriage enrichment and in crisis counseling, an explicit explanation is in order.

All close relationships function according to certain implicit ground rules and tacit agreements. In most marriages this working agreement simply develops haphazardly, in the interaction of the early years, with little conscious awareness of what the ground rules are. When there are basic differences in each person's understanding of the covenant, chronic conflict results. Contracts that were relatively fair and functional, in the early years, usually are partially unfair and out-of-date by mid-marriage. Thus, updating your marriage covenant is essential to mid-years marriage renewal.

Revising your covenant follows logically from evaluating your relationship and rethinking your priorities and values (see chapter 4). Here are the basic steps in recontracting:

1. Begin by each of you writing down your answers to the questions listed below and any other questions that are relevant to your relationship. Putting your understanding of your present working agreement *in writing* helps to clarify your own thinking. It also helps each spouse to communicate to the other their individual perceptions of their contract.

2. Discuss the similarities and differences in your understanding of your covenant.

3. Mark all the points of disagreement and the points at which either of you feels your present agreement would be improved by revision. Work through these points one by one, taking as much time as you need to negotiate a compromise or decide on changes to make your covenant now, in your present life stage, more fair and mutually fulfilling. If you get stuck in the process of negotiating, ask your pastor, or a couple you trust, to serve as a facilitator/arbitrator. Keep asking, "What is the most fulfilling approach to this issue for both of us?" In areas of conflict either both of you will win, or both of you will lose—because if only one person wins the relationship suffers.

4. Write out a joint statement of your revised and improved covenant.

5. Celebrate your accomplishment by an informal ritual of

recommitment. Do this by yourselves as a couple or in your sharing group. Some couples find it meaningful to speak their revised vows to each other, as a part of an informal love feast, a private celebration of the beginning of a new chapter in their marriage. The symbolism of feeding each other, using the elements of Communion or perhaps the segments of an orange is meaningful to many couples. Here is what one couple wrote for their moments of recommitment; each of them said to the other: "With expectation and joy, I commit myself to you—to the person you are and are becoming; I commit myself to responsibility for *my own growth* as a person; I commit myself to *us*—to our growing together as 'forever friends.' Let this food which I give to you now, be a symbol of my intention to nurture your spirit, as both of us are surrounded and fed by the Spirit of Love."

In revising and renewing their covenants many couples focus on specific areas of concern: What do I (we) expect of our marriage? What do I expect my spouse to give in our relationship? What do I expect to give? How do we share responsibility for rearing our children? How is the dirty work and the satisfying work divided? What is my understanding about each person's opportunities for developing personal talents (e.g., through further education)? Who makes the money? Who decides about spending it? How do we decide about moving? What is our agreement about friends, sex, religion, recreation, relatives (including in-laws), time to communicate? How often do we agree to reevaluate this covenant? You may wish to add questions or issues which you need to face in revising your covenant. Update your covenant in your own way, but *do* it whenever either of you feels the need for change.

This process may seem legalistic and mechanical, when one first encounters it. Some people ask, "Isn't just loving each other enough?" Regular recontracting is simply a way of strengthening the only firm foundation on hich a loving relationship can be built—justice and equality.

For years in our marriage Charlotte felt burdened by a

disproportionate share of the dirty work; I felt the full load of breadwinning. Our programming about sex roles made this division of labor seem "normal." Not until we challenged our own sex role stereotypes could we revise our contract in these areas to make it fairer to both of us.

The Intentional Marriage Method* is an excellent, low-threat tool for revising your marriage covenant to make it more mutually need-satisfying. By beginning with affirmation of what you appreciate in each other you provide a positive context for facing the unmet needs in your relationship.

Setting Up a Mid-Years Marriage Enrichment Program

In marriage enrichment, mixed-age groups are usually more feasible than groups composed exclusively of mid-years couples. It is important, within a mixed group, to offer opportunities for couples to share with other couples in their marital stage insights about handling the problems and possibilities creatively. This can be accomplished by providing opportunities for persons in similar age categories to meet occasionally in sub-groups during a retreat or ongoing group.

Some mid-years couples resist participating in marriage enrichment events because of a misconception expressed by one woman: "That sort of thing is for young people." A mid-years man responded to an invitation to participate by saying, "We're getting by. Why rock the boat?" Highly resistant or anxious couples should not, of course, be pushed. But, a personal invitation can correct misconceptions, allay anxieties, and enable couples to participate in a process which can open exciting new possibilities for them. Effective publicity—printed or oral—should affirm the positive potentials in normal marriages and the satisfactions of discovering this treasure.† Publicity should emphasize the advantages of enriching relationships regularly throughout all the stages of marriage. Couples with severely troubled marriages should be encouraged, in the publicity, to seek counseling before participating in marriage enrichment.

The best way to involve more mid-years couples in renewal

is to encourage couples clubs and classes which include mid-years people to schedule enrichment retreats once or twice a year.   Another low-threat approach is to offer enrichment opportunities in the adult education and lay training programs of a church.

Couples who experience a rebirth of their relationship through marriage enrichment often feel a desire to share with other couples what they have discovered.   Getting involved in helping to set up and perhaps lead an enrichment program in your church or community is a constructive way of sharing the good things that have happened to you.   When you do this you will find that sharing your growth is an important way to keep growing.

If you are a mid-years couple with an open, growing relationship, a love for people and an interest in helping make ordinary marriages and good marriages better, why not consider getting trained to lead marriage enrichment experiences? This can be one of the most satisfying forms of lay ministry. The training which is needed has been described elsewhere.*

Now, Create a Program

If your church needs a more effective approach to meet the enrichment needs of mid-years couples, interrupt your reading now to draw up a tentative plan. If possible, do this as a couple.   Even better, work with two or three other couples who share an interest in mid-marriage enrichment.   Together, create and implement a plan that will enable the maximum number of mid-years couples in your church and community to learn how to develop more satisfying, generative, and intentional marriages.

4. Revising Priorities and Values

Existence will remain meaningless to you if you yourself do not penetrate into it with active love and if you do not in this way discover its meaning for yourself. Meet the world with the fullness of your being and you will meet God. . . . If you wish to believe, love.*

—Martin Buber

If the mid-years are to become the good, rich years they have the potential of being, a revision of one's values and of the lifestyle they produce may be essential. This revision can be the most important but also the most difficult step one takes in responding creatively to the challenge of the mid-years. Value clarification and revision are essential ingredients in mid-years counseling and marriage enrichment.

Some of us must be stopped in our tracks by a medical or marital crisis before we take stock of our lives and our values. Years ago, while I was a hospital chaplain, I called on a man in his late forties who was slowly recuperating from a major heart attack. Reflecting on what he had gone through since the attack, he said, "For the first time in my life I've been forced to be still long enough to look at what my frantic pace has done to myself and my family." He went on to describe the sweetness of simply being alive and the changes he had made in his attitudes concerning what is really important. In retrospect, I now realize that I could not really understand what he was saying then. Not until I had a confronting hospitalization experience myself, some years later, did I begin to comprehend the agonizing reappraisal he was experiencing. Crises can often help us—even force us—to examine our lives and our values.

Fortunately, not everyone has to be floored by a major crisis before they take a careful, self-critical look at the effects of their lifestyle. A businesswoman at a mid-years enrichment workshop described her response to her fiftieth birthday: "Suddenly, it hit me—*I, Jean Carey, have a limited number of years in which to do what I want to do with my life!* In my work, when you discover you have a limited amount of capital, you rethink your investment plan!" This chapter is an invitation to rethink *your* life investment plan, and the values which determine it.

One of the assets of the mid-years is this increased awareness of the brevity and preciousness of time. Birthdays come with accelerating rapidity. A recent study of the growth stages of adulthood showed that a quiet urgency is common during the thirty-five to forty-three age group—"Time, once shrugged off as infinite, was now visibly finite and the view was worrisome."* Fortunately, this sense of urgency can create the motivation to reexamine one's life-shaping priorities and values. The pressure of this urgency continues until one makes peace with time by choosing to invest it well.

The study just cited revealed that many mid-years people reorient their values spontaneously: "They were more eager [than in the thirties] to have 'human' experiences, such as sharing the joys, sorrows, confusions, and triumphs of everyday life, rather than searching for the glamour, the glitter, the power, or the abstract. Precious moments of contact and deep feelings define the value of being in touch. Death becomes a new presence for this age group."† The growing awareness of the inevitability of death can enhance the awareness that life is very precious.

Of course, those of us in the mid-years have no corner on value struggles. Countless people in all age groups suffer from value conflicts and "value vacuums" in their inner lives.‡ Values problems are epidemic in our times. The widespread collapse of traditional certainties and value systems has created both the present value chaos and the opportunity to find life-affirming *adult* values to guide us. The time-bind and the awareness of mortality makes the value crunch even more painful for many in the mid-years. This pain is increased by the fact that faulty values and choices in the past have closed many options in the present and the future.

Lest this whole matter seem to be accompanied by funereal tones, let me reemphasize that the central reason for reappraising your lifestyle and values is not the fear of having a heart attack or suffering some other disasters. Rather it is to make sure that you are on the road you really want to travel —the road that will allow you to use the years ahead creatively, productively, and joyfully, whatever life brings. A better future is more likely to occur by choice than by chance.

The Process of Revising Your Investment Plan

There are six steps by which a couple can make a mid-course correction of their priorities and values. I will outline these steps—which can be used in counseling and enrichment sessions as well as by individual couples—and then describe some tools for implementing them.

1. Each person identifies and clarifies his or her guiding values and priorities.

2. Each person reevaluates her or his values and ranks them in a better order.

3. As spouses, compare and coordinate your respective values and priorities.

4. Devise and coordinate plans for reallocating your time and energies to move toward your revised and improved objectives. Recontracting is a part of this step and the next.

5. Implement these plans.

6. Reexamine your lifestyles periodically and make whatever further correction of direction is needed to keep you on your chosen course.

The value reorientation exercises which follow are helpful tools for implementing these six steps. The exercises may be used effectively either alone or in a group.

In a column down the left side of a sheet of paper (perhaps in your growth journal) list the ten most important things in your life. You may want to include things such as your work, family relationships, religion, health, recreation and hobbies, and your "cause."/ Now number these ten in order of their importance to you, making the thing you would most hate to lose number one./ In a column to the right of this list of values and priorities write the approximate amount of time you actually invested in each of these areas during the last two weeks (choose a longer or shorter period of time if that would be more meaningful.)/ Add to your list other less-valued activities, noting the time they consumed./

Now, check to see to what extent the ways you are actually investing your life (that is, your time) correspond to your list of priorities./ Does your allocation of time show a more honest picture of your real values and priorities than your list? Or do you need to reallocate your time and energy to invest more of yourself in the things that really matter to you? Reflect on these questions./ In another column to the right, put a plus beside the items in which you want to invest more time, and a minus beside those which deserve less./

Share your discoveries with your spouse. At what points are your and your spouse's priorities in conflict? Discuss the implications of your findings. What changes are indicated in your marriage and lifestyle?/

Now, write out plans which will enable you both to give more of yourselves to the things that matter most. This process usually requires negotiation and creative compromises in those areas in which your priorities conflict./ Integrate these changes into your revised marriage covenant (chapter 3)./

Take responsibility for implementing your side of the plans and encouraging each other in what may be a struggle to reorient your working values. Keep track, in your growth logs, of your progress toward implementation of a more intentional and value-guided lifestyle.

The process just described can help you take a candid look at how your values are affecting your life and where they are taking you. Your present allocation of time is a rough indicator of your functional values. Awareness of your actual time schedule can help you use more of your time for what you really prize. In this way you can control your schedule rather than having it control you. This exercise can be an instrument for taking back into your own hands the power you have given over to your datebook. It can help you live more intentionally.

It's safe to assume that enriching your marriage is one of your priorities or you wouldn't be reading this book. The marital checkup and covenant revision suggested in the previous chapter are ways of reevaluating and improving that important aspect of your life. If you used those tools, you are already well along in the process of making your life investment plan serve you better.

Here is a goal-oriented approach that complements the above exercise. On the left side of another sheet in your growth log, quickly list all your main goals, the things you want to achieve during the rest of your life./ Now put each goal in a time frame. Put "10 years," "5 years," "1 year," "1 month," "1 week" beside the things on your list which you want to achieve within your specified time periods./ Compare your list of goals with that of your spouse./ Together create a list of join goals for your marriage./

Now, taking one goal at a time from your list of individual goals, develop and write out workable plans for achieving each goal./ Work together with your spouse on plans for achieving your joint goals./ Keep a record of your progress toward implementation of your goals.

If these exercises seem cumbersome or mechanical to you, I recommend that you devise your own less-structured approaches to revising your life-investment plans. The books by Sidney Simons and Bryan Hall in the Annotated Bibliography describe a variety of value clarification tools which can be useful in mid-life.

Guidelines for Generative Values

The cause of much mid-years zestlessness and marital malaise is the commitment to nongenerative, inadequate values. For a couple to agree on values in a marriage won't help if the values are themselves impoverished or distorted. What is needed is a commitment to more generative values. Generative values are those which foster creativity, growth, and wholeness for others as well as oneself, indeed for all of humankind. Several women of my acquaintance (including the one to whom I am married) are experiencing the mid-years as exciting new chapters in their lives. This became possible for them only when their consciousness was raised and, as a result, they challenged many of the values to which they had committed their earlier years, values which had kept them from discovering their full intelligence and creativity. Many people have found their middle years to be an excellent time for reconsidering and reordering their values and priorities.

Here are some questions derived in part from the twelve strategies in chapter 2—which can be used to evaluate the adequacy, the generativity, of one's goals and priorities:

1. Do my (our) values and priorities, and the lifestyle they produce, allow me (us) to maintain robust physical-emotional health in the mid-years?

2. Do my (our) values and lifestyle allow me (us) time to develop my (our) mid-years potential—intellectually and spiritually? Do I take time to enjoy the satisfactions of the mind and heart? Gradually shifting one's energies from outer achievements to inner fulfillment is an essential value shift in the mid-years. Speaking to Princeton students, the late Adlai E. Stevenson once declared: "What a man knows at fifty that he did not know at twenty boils down to something like this: the knowledge that he has acquired with age is not the knowledge of formulas . . . but of people, places, actions— a knowledge not gained . . . by words, but by touch, sight, sound, victories, failures, sleeplessness, devotion, love—the human experiences and emotions of this earth; and perhaps, too, a little faith and a little reverence for the things you cannot see."* To relish and build on those fragments of insight and wisdom you have acquired by hard experience—this is the challenge of the interior life in the mid-years.

3. Do my (our) values and lifestyle allow me (us) time to enjoy the good things of life and to do the creative worthwhile and fulfilling things I (we) could do? If your values cause

you to invest too much of yourself in work, duty, and responsibility, you probably need to achieve a better balance by giving creativity and play higher priorities in your life. Midyears depression may stem from chronic hunger for more satisfaction and enjoyment.

4. Do my (our) present values and lifestyle leave me (us) enough time with the person or persons I (we) care most about? A corporation lawyer died suddenly at sixty-nine from a heart attack. His whole adult life, up to and including the day he died, had been poured into his work. His widow shared her deep regret with the friends who gathered after the funeral: "We always looked forward to having some time just for ourselves. Now it's too late."

In my experience, the most common complaint of midyears couples is this: "We want more time with each other." In these busy years it's easy to let nearly everything else, including many less important things, come before one's marriage. It behooves us to live our time fully, especially in those precious relationships that help give our existence meaning.

A friend in her mid-twenties lost her husband after an extended fight with cancer. Following his death, she wrote to her relatives and friends: "To all of you I would say (as I'm sure Mark would wish me to): live out your love for one another now. Don't assume the future; don't assume all kinds of healing time for the bruising places in your relationship with others. Don't be afraid to touch and share deeply and openly all the tragic and joyful dimensions of life."* These are wise words for any of us at any age. They are particularly appropriate for those of us in the mid-years.

5. Do my (our) values and lifestyle allow both of us to keep growing as fully as possible? Do we have equal opportunities to develop and use our potentialities? In many marriages there is commitment to roles which reflect an unequal valuing of the two persons' rights to growth and fulfillment. This inequity eventually diminishes the joy and intimacy of the relationship, even though both parties agree on the arrangement.

6. Does my (our) lifestyle reflect the most significant and life-giving values? Abraham Maslow, in his research on self-actualizing people, identified what he called "B-values" [B for Being], which guided and motivated their lives. These intrinsic values, he held, are biologically based, in that with them, people grow and stay well; without them, people get sick psychologically. These B-values are the path to a fulfilled life and a good society. Many of them are found in the major religious traditions. Some of them are emphasized in the time-tested wisdom of the Hebrew-Christian heritage. They are undergirded by the nature of the spiritual universe. Because they embody the basic principles of psychological and interpersonal reality, a commitment to these values is essential to a wholeness-tending life or marriage. Maslow lists 15 of these B-values: truth, goodness, beauty, wholeness, synergy (transformation of opposites into unities), aliveness, uniqueness, completeness, justice, order, simplicity, richness (intricacy), effortlessness, playfulness, and autonomy.*

7. Do my (our) values and lifestyle allow me (us) time for a significant cause, a challenge beyond my (our) inner circle, that will help others and improve my (our) community? We human beings have a deep need to give as well as to get love, to serve as well as to be served. As psychologist James Bugental has said: "It's as much the nature of human beings to dream the impossible dream as to scurry around for selfish gain."† Does your lifestyle allow you to dream some "impossible dream" for a better tomorrow and invest yourself in helping it become reality?

8. Are my (our) values and lifestyle consistent with sound survival value for the human family? It isn't enough to test one's values by the criterion of what will give myself, my marriage, and my family fulfillment. Such personal and family narcissism is, in the long run, self-defeating for myself and my family, because it denies our basic responsibility to the larger human family of which we all are members. Unless the majority of us in affluent countries change our greedy lifestyles of enormous consumption and waste, the children of the human

family will have an impoverished planet within a few decades. Even today, with two-thirds of our brothers and sisters around the planet malnourished, it is imperative that we alter our values and lifestyles to enable everyone on the earth to have an opportunity for a genuinely human existence.

To implement our concern for the survival of a livable planet, we must make our circles of generativity more and more inclusive. As Erik Erikson declares, "It is important for us to support the idea that a person can be generative by helping to create a world which can promise a minimum for every child born."* *Inclusive generativity* is a basic survival value. A viable lifestyle for the future must involve our investing more of our time, skills, and resources in self-transcending, family-transcending, nation-transcending commitment to helping save the biosphere and making a full life as possible for all the earth's children as it is for our own.

A robust ecological or social conscience is more essential today than ever before in the human story. We're all passengers on a tiny spaceship, planet earth. We cannot possibly continue to have a free, fulfilled life unless we learn to befriend the biosphere and to make the opportunity for a good life the birthright of every person everywhere. Erikson points out that the virtue or strength that goes with mid-years generativity is *care*. We can have a good life in the decades ahead only if we broaden our circles of caring far beyond our marriages and our family, to care for and about the whole earth and its peoples.

To measure our values and stretch our consciences by the challenge of inclusive generativity is to be faithful to the biblical vision of the good life. In that vision our caring and generativity are directed to all the children of one Creator who has made us all of one blood. The guiding vision for Christians is that of a new creation resulting from a new being —a new state of consciousness, awareness, and caring relationships on the earth. This is our calling and our commitment—a commitment that is the path to wholeness for ourselves, our families, and the family of humankind.

5. Methods of Spiritual Enrichment and Inner Renewal

Among all my patients in the second half of life—that is to say, over 35—there has not been one whose problem in the last resort was not that of finding a religious outlook on life.*
—Carl Gustav Jung

Spiritual enrichment and inner renewal are important ways of increasing mid-years creativity. They are an essential foundation on which to develop a more mutually-enlivening marriage. This is an area in which ministers have unique and essential contributions to make in marriage counseling and renewal.

Inner poverty is a common cause of marital boredom and conflict. Alienation from oneself always produces distancing in relationships. I have noticed in myself that whenever I get disconnected from my inner space, or allow it to become cramped or cluttered, my close relationships suffer, as do my teaching, counseling, and writing. Taking time to reconnect with my center and to make this inner space a better place to be "at home" has salutary effects on these relationships and activities.

John Gardner states pointedly the danger of inner deadness: " 'Keep on growing,' the commencement speakers say, 'Don't go to seed. Let this be a beginning, not an ending.' It is a good theme. Yet a high proportion of the young people who hear the speeches pay no heed and by the time they are middle-aged they are absolutely mummified."† Mummified mid-years marriages both reflect and increase inner mummification. Marital resurrection is possible, beginning with re-vitalization within each of the partners.

Increasing the spiritual sharing in a marriage deepens the care and intimacy of that relationship. "Quite apart from any churchy or churchly considerations, the spiritual dimension of a marriage is a source of food for spiritual growth and health. ... The moments of sharing on the spiritual level are tender, precious moments in a relationship."* Such moments become increasingly important and wholeness-giving in the second half of a marriage.

This chapter aims at helping increase the aliveness and enjoyment of inner space—the place where each of us is most with ourself and from which we reach out to others. Numerous methods are available now for the spiritual-intellectual growth work which produces inner renewal. In the following pages, I will describe several of these methods which have been helpful to me and to mid-years persons with whom I have counseled and shared enrichment experiences. I hope these methods will encourage you to discover other ways as well for enriching the vertical dimensions of your life and your marriage. I suggest that you try each method with your spouse to discover if it works for you. Remember, spiritual growth is contagious. Spiritual growth in others is best facilitated by persons who are themselves growing.

Communicating About What Matters Most

Marriage partners can stimulate and support each other's inner renewal by taking time to talk regularly about their real concerns. Sharing your intellectual, spiritual, and value struggles can encourage each other's spiritual growth and strengthen vertical dimension intimacy.

To practice this kind of communication, find a quiet place and take turns, as a couple, completing the following sentences. Take them one at a time, spending as much time as you need to discuss thoroughly the issues and feelings that arise: "The ideas and issues which excite me most are . . .;" "The things that are most worth living for right now are . . .;" "I feel the most joy (pain, hope, lonely, together) when . . .;" "What I really believe about God is . . .;" "I feel closest to (most distant from) God when . . .;" "I get spiritually high when . . .;" "The beliefs that mean the most to me now are . . .;" "The beliefs from my childhood which no longer make sense are . . .;" "Life has the least (the most) meaning for me when . . .;" "I feel closest to you (most distant from you) spiritually when . . .;" "The way I really feel about the church is . . .;" "I'd like to do the following, to enjoy more spiritual sharing . . .;" "To enrich the spiritual life of our family, I'd like to . . .;" "Other things about our spiritual growth that concern me are . . .;" "The way I feel about discussing these questions is . . ."

If you haven't talked about such matters as these for a long time, or ever, it may be difficult or embarrassing at first. But with practice, sharing on this level can become deeply satisfying.

Intellectual Renewal

Research shows that if you continue to exercise your mind, your intellectual powers can be at their peak during the middle years.* The energies and creativity of your mind will continue at a high level long after your body has slowed down, if you keep using it. To love God with your mind means to *use* your mind—that marvelous, mysterious, creative gift of God—as fully and productively as possible, throughout your life.

An educated person is one who *enjoys* using her or his mind in lifelong learning.† The mid-years offer fresh opportunities to learn what *you* really want to know (in contrast to what others think you should know). It's a time to enjoy acquiring a new skill, hobby, or language. My best friend always wanted to know more about philosophy and the history of ideas. Now in her early fifties, she has completed her doctorate in that area. She's excited by the discoveries of new mind-stretching truths. Psychiatrist Robert N. Butler, in discussing creativity in the later years, declares that the goal of these years is to become an "autodidact"—literally, a self-teacher.‡ Without a doubt, your mind has rich undeveloped and underdeveloped capacities. Allow yourself to enjoy the adventure of discovering these inner powers.

Here's an intentional approach to intellectual renewal. Begin by listing in your growth journal all the subjects, issues, and problems you'd really like to know more about./ List all the skills you'd enjoy having. Compare your lists with those of your partner. See if there are areas of shared interest./ Select one of these areas to develop together./ Now each of you also pick an interest to develop on your own./ Decide what books, seminars, people, courses, and other resources will help you explore the issues or acquire the skills you have chosen as your personal and your shared growth goals./ Write out workable plans for moving ahead in widening your own mental horizons and enriching your intellectual intimacy.

Meditation for Inner Refreshment

The hectic pace of the mid-years makes it essential to develop effective methods of centering—ways of contacting and renewing one's inner space. Many persons are discovering that the techniques of meditation help them experience regular inner refreshment. One busy mid-years couple reports that the two periods they spend meditating each day gives them a tonic for tensions as well as other rewards which far surpass their investment of time.* Research studies reveal that various forms of meditation and relaxation produce significant changes in body chemistry, blood pressure, and oxygen consumption that probably benefit physical, mental, and spiritual health.† Meditative techniques are excellent ways of enlivening one's devotional and prayer experiences.

I find that *meditation breaks* help me rest my hyperactive mental motor and renew my inner energies. Charlotte has encouraged me in my efforts to develop regular contact with my "serenity zone," by being willing to share her longer experience with meditation.‡

Here are some guidelines for meditating, derived from her approach and various other sources. I suggest that you try them now. While standing, relax your body by tensing and releasing all your muscles three or four times./ Now sit in a comfortable, straight-backed chair, in a quiet place, in whatever posture allows you not to be preoccupied with your body. After you read the following guidelines, close your eyes and practice them for fifteen to twenty minutes. Take several deep breaths, allowing your tensions to flow out as you exhale./ Focus your attention on your breathing. Be aware of its continuing inflow-outflow, inflow-outflow. Notice that the air is cooler as it flows in, warmer as it flows out./ Become one with your breathing.

Don't try to achieve any particular mental state or goal. This form of meditation aims at the opposite of trying to *achieve.* Let go. Flow with your experience wherever it carries you. Each time you exhale, try repeating over and over, one word or a short phrase which feels comfortable to your mind. Concentrating on one sound may help you *center* your consciousness by quieting the inner conversations and interrupting the tumbling stream of feelings and thoughts. I find that the inner sound of "one," or "peace," or "shalom," or "warm," helps me quiet and experience my consciousness. Pick a word, perhaps, from your religious traditions, which has a good feeling for you, but not one which will trigger a theological discussion within your mind.

It may also help you to center if you form and focus on a picture or image back of your closed eyelids—perhaps a rose, a snowflake, a sunset, a cross, a star of David, a mandala. Try different sounds and/or images, until you find one sound or image, or a combination of a sound and image, that helps you achieve refreshing quietness within. If thoughts, outside sounds, or itches occur, don't fret or fight them. Just observe them passing through your consciousness. Continue to focus on your breathing and your centering sound and/or image.

The meditative state is somewhere between ordinary waking consciousness and sleep, but it is different from both. It varies for each person and on different occasions. Occasionally it may bring feelings of transcendence or ecstasy. Research evidence shows that salutary bodily effects often occur, even when the subjective experience doesn't seem particularly helpful. Most people find that, with practice, meditation provides refreshing oases in their day.

Over a period of several weeks try meditating twice a day, before meals, for about twenty minutes. If you find that you have trouble disciplining yourself to meditate twice daily, a training course in Transcendental Meditation or some other approach may increase your motivation. Share and learn from each other's experiences with meditation.

Enriching Your Inner Space

Meditation brings inner renewal by opening you to the deeper resources of your consciousness. Active imaging is a complementary method of inner enrichment.

For example, try closing your eyes and picturing your consciousness as a space or a room within yourself./ Now expand your consciousness by pushing back the walls of your inner room, or change it in other ways to make it a better place to be at home./ Now, imagine that you are opening yourself to let warmth and light flow into your inner space and your whole body—the warmth and light of God's healing, energizing Spirit./ As the warmth and light fill you, let them flow out through your hands, to blend with the warmth and light of your spouse and surround you both./ Continue this for at least ten minutes./ Now, discuss your experience with your spouse./ Experiment with other images to enrich your inner world./

Developing Your "Other Side"

As Carl Jung made clear, inner wholeness, particularly after age forty, usually requires developing one's neglected "other side"—the soft, nurturing, feelingful, vulnerable side in a man and the strong, assertive, analytical side in a woman. Our culture's narrow sex-role stereotypes encourage us to ignore or reject these rich, balancing sides of ourselves. The spiritual lopsidedness which results becomes increasingly limiting in the second half of life. By claiming their neglected sides, a couple enhances the inner resources which each brings to their marriage. They can appreciate and enjoy more dimensions of each other's personhood, thus increasing their intimacy in relating.

Befriending the so-called feminine and masculine sides in oneself and one's partner can also facilitate spiritual enrichment by increasing each person's openness to the nurturing, comforting, and confronting-ethical sides of religious experience. Our spiritual health is enhanced by thus keeping the maternal and the paternal sides of our experiences of God in balance.

A couple can help each other develop increased inner wholeness by affirming more liberated, whole behavior when it occurs. A husband's appreciation of his wife's assertiveness, and a wife's appreciation of her husband's soft, nurturing behavior, can help each accept and develop these sides of themselves.*

Open Yourself to Peak Experiences

Because life in the mid-years often becomes dull and two-dimensional, energizing moments of transcendence are vital to renewal. Psychologist Abraham Maslow regarded such moments as "peak experiences," little moments of self-actualization which are one of the ways we grow.† He regarded these little mystical moments as life-validating in that they make life worthwhile and unified. They are "integrative of the splits within the person, between persons, . . . and between the person and the world."‡

One cannot create such spiritual highs. They are a normal part of life and experience, but a part we often ignore. Our task is to become more aware of and open to them, and more able to celebrate them when they occur. Slowing down our pace, and increasing our experience of the "now" through meditation, can enhance our awareness of the moments of uplift which are easily overlooked in our hectic lives and inner dullness.

These precious moments often occur in commonplace

events. It increases my awareness of a special moment if I pause within myself when it occurs and simply let myself enjoy the experience. Later, I may write the letters P.E. (peak experience) beside the jotting I've made about it in my personal log. In plateau times, when life goes flat, it helps to return to these jottings and enjoy reliving the peak experience of a child's smile, a breathtaking sunset, a moving encounter with a person, a sexual high, a majestic strain of music, a feeling of connectedness with the flow of life and with the Spirit of the universe.

So let yourself savor these mountaintop moments; let yourself relive the lift and the gratitude you felt for the gift of transcendence. Share peak experiences with each other. Enliven your marriage spiritually by finding more experiences which give you peaks together.*

I am writing this during the week before Easter. As I once again experience within myself the drama of these special days, I am moved by the power of the inner experience of Easter. All growth is a process of death and resurrection, which means that growth involves struggle, risk, and pain. Before any of us can be reborn to more open, loving marriages, some of the self-absorption and defensiveness that distances us from each other must die. The good news is that resurrection to new aliveness and new relationships is possible!

Psychiatrist Fritz Kunkel, in his discussion of the "continuing creation," declares: "Easter, rebirth, the new creation, is either a convincing inner experience which changes our character and our lives, or it is nothing at all. . . . Creative power fills our souls. . . . Life and Light and Love begin anew."† To witness continuing creation in a person or in a relationship is a profoundly moving peak experience. When I see it happening in an enrichment group or a counseling session, I know that I am indeed standing on holy ground.

Peak experiences are invaluable resources for handling constructively the accelerating losses of the mid-years. These experiences can increase awareness of the larger context of

one's life. In these fleeting moments of rebirth to larger dimensions of self, relationships, and the Spirit, something of the
larger life becomes experiential. My brief, fragile life is part
of an ongoing creative process—part of a reality in which I
can participate and which will continue after I am gone. In
my participation in this process I transcend my puny, time-
and nature-bound existence. I belong! I am a small but
significant part of the larger life!

Putting Away Childish Things

One of the blocks which prevents persons from enjoying
more spiritual adventure and transcendence is the cold inner
lump of unfaced doubts, obsolete beliefs, and fossilized fears
of God left from childhood. Reducing this logjam helps clear
the inner channels for the flow of spiritual energies. Letting
go of the childish feelings we project on the universe can release us to experience the reality of the energizing Spirit of
growth and love. The realism and spiritual hunger of the mid-
years can give one courage to risk letting go of obsolete beliefs.

Here is a method of doing this spiritual maturation work.
Try it with your spouse or in a spiritual growth group.

In your growth journal, list the religious beliefs, attitudes,
and practices which make sense to you intellectually and are
important in your present life./ Discuss the list with your
partner and/or your group./ Now list the religious beliefs,
attitudes, and practices which no longer seem valid or important, even though you still go through the motions of paying
them lip service./ Discuss these with your spouse and/or
group./

Getting the things you affirm, and those you don't, out in
the open can help you let go of leftover spiritual baggage.
This lets you reinvest your spiritual energies in growth-
producing adult faith and values. Childish beliefs often have
scary, irrational feeling associated with them. At first you
may feel as though you're losing your faith, when actually
you're just allowing it to grow up.

If do-it-yourself methods don't lighten your load, get the help of a competent pastoral counselor trained in the skills of a coach-facilitator of spiritual growth. Your personal religion can be a weight on your spirit, or it can give your spirit wings. Putting away childish things can release you to let yourself frolic and fly spiritually.

Renewing Basic Trust

Periodic renewal of the inner springs of trust helps enrich the mid-years spiritually. The conviction that life is basically trustworthy, in spite of its pain and disappointments, under-girds a trust-full marriage.* Unfortunately, most of us oper-ate on the basis of gut-level, works-righteousness theology. Our lives are driven by the hope that if we keep conforming, pleasing others, trying to achieve, obeying the "shoulds," per-haps someday we will feel accepted within ourselves. A driven lifestyle stemming from this illusory hope reaches a point of diminished or negative returns in the mid-years. The awareness dawns gradually that the works-righteousness path cannot lead to self-acceptance and renewed trust.

To find a better path requires that you *experience* love, the love you do not have to earn because it is simply there, al-ready there, in the relationship itself. In traditional Christian language this kind of love is called "grace." To experience grace in relationships—with one's spouse, one's spiritual search group, one's counselor—is to experience growth, heal-ing, and trust renewal. Such experiences help to make us aware of the good—the image of God—within us. They help us to "accept ourselves as being accepted" at our center.† The accepting love of others thus becomes a channel through which the loving Spirit—the source of trust and growth—can enter and renew our inner lives. As Martin Buber put it: "The extended lives of relations meet in the external Thou. Every particular Thou is a glimpse through to the eternal Thou."‡

6. Enhancing Mid-Years Sex

Like good wine, sexuality as it matures can be better and richer, if people know how to use it.*
—Beryl and Avinoam Chernick

Neither men or women lose either sexual needs or sexual function with age. . . . Given an attractive and receptive partner, decent general health and an absence of the belief that one ought to run out of steam, active sex lasts as long as life. . . . There is little if any physical decline in any attribute except frequency up to 75 and beyond.†
—Alex Comfort

An important part of enriching mid-years marriages is helping couples to increase and diversify their shared pleasures. Enhancing the enjoyment of mid-years sex is a significant ingredient in developing a couple's pleasure potential. (The fact that you're probably reading this chapter first is an indication of *how* important it is to you.) Lusty, full-bodied sex can be like sharing a refreshing drink on a dusty journey.

The findings of the sexologists, the scientists who study human sexuality, confirm what many mature couples already knew—that good sex can continue indefinitely as a tender, love-nurturing form of sharing. The studies show conclusively that "if you use it you won't lose it!"‡ A recent survey of the sexual practices of a cross-section of Americans found that couples 45 to 54 had a median figure for frequency of "making love" of 52 times a year; those 55 and up only dropped to 49 times a year.§ When Alfred Kinsey did his studies some 25 years earlier, the median for couples over 54 was only 26 times a year. The fact that all couples over 44, in the recent study, had a median frequency of intercourse of almost once a week, shows that there's a lot of life left in that age group!

The recent survey found no evidence that increased sexual liberation has produced sexual boredom as some have suggested (or hoped) it would. Rather, a new recreational attitude regarding sex has developed in our society. Sex is now widely regarded as a valuable form of play. This attitude now coexists alongside the traditional romantic view of sex. The survey showed that couples are not only doing it more but also enjoying it more. For example, the number of married women who have orgasms "never or only sometimes" declined from 28 percent in Kinsey's survey to only 15 percent. Those who have orgasms "all or almost all the time" rose from 45 percent in Kinsey's study to 53 percent in the recent study.*

Liberating Mid-Years Sex

Here are some do-it-yourselves ways by which couples can increase the sparkle in their marriage. They are methods for making ordinary and good sex better. These guidelines, developed by Charlotte and myself, have proved helpful in marriage enrichment and also in counseling couples with problems of diminished sexual pleasure. I suggest that you discuss and try them as a couple.

1. Liberate your attitudes about sex. Sexual responsiveness starts in your head, rather than your genitals, so that's the place to start enhancing sex. Begin by letting go of the negative myths and replace them with the facts about mid-years sex. Two prevalent myths are the "fading fast" myth which holds that anyone over forty-five is on the skids sexually; and the "over the hill" myth which believes that sex normally ends between sixty and sixty-five. If you believe these patently untrue myths, your anxiety can inhibit full sexual fulfillment. As suggested above, the fact is that the majority of mid-years and older couples continue enjoying sex. Some even "perfect the art of lovemaking to new levels of satisfaction."†

It is possible for most couples with healthy marriages to improve their sex life. It is probably "normal," for those who grew up in our culture during the time when those in the mid-years did, to have some hang-ups about sex. Within a relationship of mutual caring, old inhibiting attitudes gradually can be unlearned and sex-affirmative attitudes and pleasuring skills can be learned in their place, using some of the methods suggested in this chapter.

Many couples find it freeing to read together a book which suggests ways of increasing the adventure and playfulness of sex—for example, those by Alex Comfort, James McGary, and the Hunts in the Bibliography. The chapter on "Increasing Sexual Intimacy" in *The Intimate Marriage* and the chapter on "Liberated Sex" in *Meet Me in the Middle* suggest attitudes and approaches which can enliven mid-years sex.

We human beings are the most highly sexed species in the entire animal kingdom. Contrary to old dual-standard stereotypes, women have at least as rich pleasure potentials as men. The sex researchers have confirmed that many women are able to have a series of orgasms, given adequate stimulation, with only a few seconds between. Furthermore, the center of a woman's sexual arousal, the clitoris, has no known function except as a source of pleasure. These facts have profound implications for an affirmative theology of sex, pointing as they do to the way we are made psychologically and physiologically.

2. *Keep your total relationship growing and sex will tend to improve.* Sex is a powerful form of communication. Whatever enriches other dimensions of communication in a relationship usually enhances sex. A major cause of disappointment and bitterness, and therefore of sexual unresponsiveness among mid-years women, is the lack of companionship and sharing in their marriages. The foundation for the best sex you can achieve is active commitment to live as fully as you can and to help your partner do the same. Become better companions, by sharing numerous facets of your lives, and better sex will tend to follow. Sex researcher Virginia Johnson declares: "Nothing good is going to happen in bed between a husband and a wife unless good things have been happening

between them before they got into bed. There is no way for a good sexual technique to remedy a poor emotional relationship."*

Don't expect sex to be beautiful if either of you feels exploited, cheated, or unfulfilled in the marriage. As Abraham Maslow once observed, those who feel whole and self-actualized seem to enjoy all the vitalities of life more robustly. This is why the most beneficial developments sexually, for both men and women, will be the achievement of full equality of women and the full liberation of both women and men.† Two liberated, fulfilled people in bed naturally have liberated, fulfilling sex. However, during the transition period, when couples are struggling to achieve a more equalitarian relationship, many have increased problems sexually.

It's important to lower the wall and get connected emotionally by communicating openly before you try to make love. A wall of unresolved hurts, frustrations, and resentments between a couple will diminish and eventually dam up the flow of loving, sensual feelings. In our relationship, we find that having a regular time to deal with any negative feelings which have accumulated is essential. Otherwise, in spite of a mutual longing for sexual intimacy, lingering hurts and anger drive us apart or rob sex of its richness.

To keep your relationship and your self-esteem healthy, feed each other's heart hungers for affirmation regularly. For example, try completing the sentence, "I appreciate in you . . ." as many times as you can to each other, thus sharing a feast of mutual affirmation. Be sure to include the things you find sexually attractive and arousing in your "appreciates," but don't limit your affirmation to these. You may discover, as many couples do, that this exercise (from the Intentional Marriage Method) turns you on sexually.‡

Committing yourself to *positive fidelity* can enrich your total relationship and with it, your sex life. Negative fidelity is motivated primarily by guilt and fear. Positive fidelity, in contrast, is based on prizing the relationship and choosing not to jeopardize or damage this precious human bond. Positive fidelity is an essential expression of commitment to each other's full growth. It helps create the trust, continuity, and caring that is the best context for the most satisfying sex of which a couple is capable. In their book, *The Pleasure Bond*, William Masters and Virginia Johnson declare: "Total commitment, in which all sense of obligation is linked to mutual feelings of loving concern, sustains a couple sexually over the years. . . . When carrying the inescapable burdens that come with a family and maturity, they can turn to each other for the physical comforting and emotional sustenance they need to withstand economic and social pressures that often threaten to drain life of all joy."*

3. Discover and enjoy the special romance and new meanings that are possible in mid-years sex. Contrary to Hollywood stereotypes, youth have no corner on romance or passion. There's a type of romance that's available at *each* stage of marriage. Many mid-years couples find that sex has a mellow richness as it is seasoned by years of sharing and by the finesse which grows with long experience. Couples who have an ongoing romance are those who continue, in more relaxed and low-key ways, the tender thoughtfulness and caring of courtship. As the heaviest demands of child rearing diminish, and as freedom from worry about unwanted pregnancies comes with menopause, couples can enjoy a flowering of sensuality.

Psychiatrist Robert Butler points out that older couples frequently perfect the neglected "second language of sex"—the language of touching, caressing, tenderness, and leisurely erotic play.† Developing this second language enriches sex at any stage of marriage. The mid-years and beyond offer many opportunities for cultivating and enjoying this sensual art.

It's important to discover that less frequent sex doesn't necessarily mean less enjoyable sex. It may, in fact, be just the opposite. Making love with an experienced, liberated partner who can affirm both her or his sexuality and yours, is qualitatively a deeply satisfying experience, an experience that can have a unique and changing meaning for each couple throughout their years together.‡

4. Create new ways to let your inner "Child" sides play. Good sex, in Transactional Analysis terms, requires turning off the inner Parent and turning on one's playful Child.* This involves forgetting, for a while, the schedules, responsibilities, and duties which often weigh heavily in the mid-years. Turning on one's inner Child is difficult if teenage children (who are very skillful in activating our Parent side) are still in the house. It takes planning and ingenuity, but it's possible to schedule regular mini-vacations, brief periods to let your Child sides frolic together. A night at an attractive motel, an afternoon at the beach, dinner out with an opportunity to linger over candlelight—these are examples of mini-vacations that can liberate the fun-loving inner Child and thus enable satisfying sex. One busy couple we know sets aside two hours each week for a mutual "pleasuring session." The husband and wife take turns deciding and planning these sessions.

By using your imagination, it's possible to introduce variety and adventure into your sexual experience and to reeroticize the setting. Experiment with new settings, or add sensual touches to your usual setting—for example some "music to make love by," candlelight, or perhaps an extra mirror in your bedroom. One advantage of the empty nest is that it's possible to spread out a foam rubber mat in front of the den or living room fireplace, put some sensual music on the stereo, or have the TV or radio on, if you like a little simulated exhibitionism while making love.

5. Discover what you enjoy most and coach each other on how to give maximum mutual enjoyment. Each of us has our unique pleasure preferences. Explore and experiment to discover yours. Find out what scents, caresses, words, pictures, positions, approaches, and settings best give you those luxurious feelings of arousal.

Then, since few of us are married to mind readers, do some explicit mutual coaching. Devote time to learning exactly how to make the other feel wonderful. Have a "tell and show" session, periodically, in which you describe and then guide each other's hands, mouths, and bodies so that sex play will be fully pleasurable for both of you. Work out sounds, hand signals, or words which communicate the all-important message, "That feels tremendous!   Do it some more!"   It's important for the woman to let the man know exactly when she's ready and eager for him to enter and, later, when she's ready for him to climax.

Knowledge of the four stages of lovemaking identified by Masters and Johnson can be used to enhance enjoyment: (1) Excitement stage.   This involves the opportunity for leisurely love play which slowly builds arousal.   (2) Orgasmic plateau stage.   This is the level of arousal from which one can climax with slight additional stimulation.   It may be helpful for the man to caress the woman's genital area, manually or orally, to help her reach this level of excitement.   Many men over fifty-five need direct stimulation of the penis to get it up.   After entry, by lying together quietly after each burst of action, the climax can be delayed and the passionate closeness of the plateau stage greatly prolonged.   (3) Orgasm stage.   This is more apt to be good for both if you discover a position that leaves the woman's clitoris free from the man's full weight. (4) Resolution stage.   This can be a period of the shared warmth and closeness of the afterglow.   If the woman hasn't had an orgasm, she may enjoy having the man bring her to climax manually or with a vibrator.

6. Enjoy leisurely nondemanding pleasuring.   If either of you is having trouble being as sexually responsive as you would like to be, this is probably the most important suggestion for you.   Nondemand pleasuring is one key to increasing sexual zest in a marriage where sex has become dull or flat.

Here is one approach to a nondemand pleasuring session. When you feel connected emotionally, set aside at least 1½ hours to give each other a full body massage.   Use warm body lotion with an aroma you both like.   Start with the back of your partner's neck, gradually working down to caress the feet.   Then do your partner's front, saving the genitals until last.   Relax and enjoy receiving and giving each other pleasure for its own sake, not as a preliminary to achieving any other goal (such as an orgasm).   Let go of the "we try harder" pressure on yourselves. Just flow with the natural pleasures of your bodies. Let this flow carry you wherever it will. Whatever happens will be satisfying, in all likelihood, partly because you don't have to "make it." Regular sessions of low-key nondemand pleasuring are effective ways of reawakening the springs of mid-years' passion.

Remember, "good sex" for you is whatever you both enjoy! Affirm this fact and resist the temptation to feel that what you like is substandard or abnormal. If you both like it, it's right for you. Feel free to ignore what books say (including this one) if it does not work for you, or fit your preferences and sensitivities. You are the only real expert on your own sex life. Relax and enjoy whatever is satisfying for both of you. As someone has said, "there are no winners in the bedroom olympics."*

7. Avoid the triple traps of hurry, fatigue, and too much alcohol. These three things, along with the pressure to "succeed" in the bedroom, most often interfere with satisfying mid-years sex. Hurry and fatigue are closely linked. In the early years of marriage, most of us have the youthful stamina to enjoy regular late-night sex after everything else is done. But in the mid-years and beyond, avoiding such rush and fatigue become increasingly important to good sex. Occasional spontaneous "quickies" can be fun. But when they're the result of fatigue and rush, they're the equivalent of gulping a delicious meal so fast you hardly taste the food. A relaxed Saturday morning, Sunday afternoon, or an early evening devoted to leisurely pleasuring, is much more likely to be deeply satisfying than brief, late-night intercourse.

A little alcohol helps some couples turn off their Parent sides and turn on their inner Child. But heavy drinking tends to interfere with erections and orgasms, particularly in the mid-years. The decision to drink less or not to drink at all before sex can often lead to increased enjoyment.

Many mid-years men experience occasional episodes of temporary impotence. Reducing alcohol consumption and fatigue, and shifting to nondemanding pleasuring for a while (to reduce the anxiety about failure and the pressure to succeed) usually restores fully the ability to function. Recognizing that this "problem" happens to many of us, and that it's usually nothing more than a passing episode, reduces the panic of feeling that one is "losing one's manhood."

8. If do-it-yourself methods such as those described above do not enhance your sex life sufficiently, get the help of a trained sex therapist who is also trained in marriage counseling. This is an appropriate step for those with any *chronic* sexual problem. Because sexual and emotional problems always intertwine, it's important to have a therapist who is trained to help in both areas. It's a sign of strength to recognize your need for expert help and to get it.

The Illustrated Manual of Sex Therapy by Helen Singer Kaplan describes sex therapy and also includes drawings of the erotic pleasuring positions used in such therapy. This book can be useful for any couples who wish to learn non-demand pleasuring to enhance sex for themselves. It is also a useful resource for ministers and others who do marriage counseling and enrichment.

As a kind of game, jot down quickly in your growth log all the things you can think of that turn your partner on. Now, check each other's lists to see how accurate your knowledge of each other is. Add things that you didn't think of to each of your lists. Now, together, plan a pleasuring session or mini-vacation for yourselves, using your knowledge of each other's pleasure preferences. Have fun!

7. Creative Approaches to Mid-Years Parenting and the Empty Nest

> The art of living does not consist in preserving and clinging to a particular mode of happiness, but allowing happiness to change its form . . . for happiness, like a child, must be allowed to grow up.*
>
> —Charles L. Morgan

In no area of mid-years life is the growth approach more important, or more difficult to apply, than in the area of parenting. A couple at an enrichment weekend put it well. The husband declared, "Nothing causes more hassling between us than our two teenagers." The wife added, "Yes, and when they're not stirring things up, one of our parents needs something urgently." The interlocking of the generations becomes increasingly intrusive in the mid-years. Couples feel the crunch of being in the middle between the needs of still-dependent adolescents and aging parents. Their marriages can flourish only if they learn to handle these pressures.

This chapter will suggest some ways of coping with the problems and realizing the rich possibilities of mid-years parenting and the empty nest. The approaches and methods here suggested can be used as resources by individual parents and by ministers and other leaders in planning parent training groups and marriage enrichment events.

Keep Open and Growing

Parents' most important contribution to their children's growth is to be growing people with growing marriages. Lifestyles are contagious. Adolescents who have open, affirming, pro-life parents usually "catch" something of their love of life.

As parents, you'll be more able to give your teenagers space to grow, releasing them to become autonomous adults, if you have full lives and a satisfying marriage and/or other relationships. Enriching your lives and your marriage lets you have more to give to your children and less reason to envy them.

Some Guidelines for Parents of Teens

It is relatively easy to lose one's objectivity, to get bogged down in problems, and to miss the opportunity to enjoy pleasures relating to adolescents. Here are some guidelines for helping you make your relationship with them constructive and mutually satisfying.

Keep Affirming Your Teenagers.

Tell them what you sincerely like and appreciate in them. A three-step method for resolving conflicts constructively consists of: (1) telling each other what you appreciate; (2) telling each other what you each need; and (3) negotiating a better plan to meet as many of both sets of needs as possible This adaptation of the Intentional Marriage Method* can be used in an individual family communication session, and in family clusters, camps, and counseling. It is especially important to affirm your teenagers whenever they function in ways that are creative, responsible, and responsive to other people's needs. It's not easy for youth to move into adulthood in this time of conflicting values and rapid social change. Your appreciation of their small, tentative steps in that direction can encourage them to risk moving further toward responsible adulthood.

Take time to communicate with and, if possible, to enjoy your teenagers. Because most parents and teens have hectic schedules, it's easy for them to become like "ships that pass in the night" for extended periods of time. Such parallel living may produce feelings of alienation on both sides. Taking time to relate to your adolescents in good times helps balance and keep a healthier perspective on the inevitable times of distancing and conflict.

Make Your Way of Relating to Them Increasingly Adult-to-Adult.

Gradually relax the limits and the discipline to give them room to develop self-discipline and autonomy. Be firm on B-values (such as justice and truth). Make sure the family rules are flexible and negotiable on other, less important matters. Growing into responsible adulthood involves exercising one's right to learn by making one's own mistakes. Most teenagers have to "leave home," emotionally as well as physically, before they develop the ability to relate to parents as adults. One of the pleasures of mid-years parenthood is the new and mutually satisfying relationship with young adult children who have established their autonomous identity.

Let go of the False Assumption That You Are Entirely to Blame for All Your Children's Problems.

It's a difficult time in history to be parents of adolescents. Many factors other than what you have done, not least of all their own choices, influence your adolescents' decisions. Wallowing in guilt tends to increase the hurt done by the mistakes one actually made. You probably have given your adolescents "the strength to survive your mistakes."* It may help to remind oneself that behind much teenage behavior that disturbs us adults there is a positive search. Their search is for genuine self-esteem, autonomy, for acceptance by peers, for authentic relations with other people, and for a sense of meaning and purpose in their lives. In short, teenagers are in the midst of a painful but hopeful identity struggle.

When the Inevitable Crises Arise, Don't Panic.

Whatever you do, don't rupture the relationship by heavy-handed or manipulative methods. When one is most tempted to be heavy-handed is precisely the time when your teens need a caring, supportive relationship with you most. If communication breaks down, get the help of a trained family counselor. Such a person can be both referee and coach in helping your family remobilize its own resources for resolving the conflicts constructively.†

Find a Parent Training and Enrichment Group.

Coping with the problems and developing the positive potentialities of parent-teen relationships will be facilitated if parents do not try to go it alone but instead, find a support group of other parents. Joining the local ACME (Association of Couples for Marriage Enrichment) group is an effective way of discovering couples who are interested in enriching their own marriages and in providing increased opportunities for others to do so. If an ACME group doesn't exist yet in your area, their national office will provide you with guidance in starting one.*

Marriage enrichment events involving mid-marrieds should provide opportunities for these couples to share ways of strengthening relations with their adolescents. A mid-years couples class can have a series focused on "creative parenting" using a book on family communication such as Virginia Satir's *Peoplemaking.*† Parent Effectiveness Training and other parent education approaches can be helpful to parents of adolescents.‡ Transgenerational communication events are workshops in which parents and teens take part in communication exercises designed to build bridges across the generation gap.§ "Family clusters," composed of three or four families plus several singles, can provide mutual caring, enrichment, learning and communication among several families and between adolescents and adults who are not their parents.‖ Solo parents face a special challenge when their children reach adolescence. It's important for them to find or develop a support group to provide mutual encouragement and companionship for themselves, and opportunities for their adolescents to relate to other caring adults of both sexes.

Changing Your Inner Responses

Enjoying your teenagers and relating to them creatively will be more feasible if, in the language of Transactional Analysis, you first make peace with your inner Parent; enjoy, befriend, and control your inner Adolescent; and keep your inner Adult in the driver's seat when you communicate with your teenagers.* In addition to the three parts of the personality described in T.A. literature—Parent, Adult, Child—there is also that fourth part of every adult's personality, the inner Adolescent he or she once was. Our inner Adolescent is reactivated by the presence of teenagers. Most parents are not aware of this influence even when their inner Adolescent is distorting their responses to their flesh-and-blood teenagers. Much of the painful, unproductive conflict between parents and teenagers results from the teenagers' activating or "hooking" their parents' inner Adolescent.

Getting to know, like, and control your inner Adolescent can enable you to do the same with your actual teenagers. As you have made peace with the Parent you carry within you, you will be able to relate more appropriately to your teenagers because your inner Adolescent will not need to be either submissive or defiant. To illustrate, being overpermissive or overpunishing with teenagers is usually the result of conflicts between the parent's inner Adolescent and inner Parent.

Keeping one's inner Adult in control in relating to one's teenagers is easier said than done, of course. Here's an awareness exercise that can help parents meet and come to terms with their inner Child, Adolescent, and Parent.

Close your eyes and become aware of your body and of your inner space./ Picture in your mind the house where you lived as a child and see yourself at that age inside the house. Be aware of the feelings of the child./ Picture your parents joining the child, one at a time; watch what happens. How does each feel?/ Now, let the years pass and see yourself as an adolescent in the house where you lived then. What are your feelings as an adolescent?/ Picture your parents joining you, one at a time; see what happens./ Recall and relive the feelings of several incidents from your teens—experiences involving punishment, approval, peers, sex, religion, alcohol./ If your memories are mainly of pain and alienation, see if you can have your adolescent self and your parents come together and be reconciled in your inner picture./ Relive the time when you left home and said good-bye to your parents. Be aware of the feelings on both sides./ If your inner adolescent is sad, lonely, or lacking in self-esteem, picture yourself as an adult, comforting and encouraging her or him./ Be aware of the strength of your Adult, the here-and-now part of you which can choose not to be controlled by your inner Child, Adolescent, or Parent./ Now, complete your memory journey in any way you choose and, when you are done, open your eyes./ Discuss with your spouse your experience of exploring the past./

I hope that this exercise helped you get better acquainted with your inner Child, Adolescent, and Parent sides and made you more aware of the ability of your Adult to control their influences. Did you become more aware of ways in which your feelings and attitudes from your early life influence your relationships with your teenagers?

Parents as Pioneers

Margaret Mead has observed that parents of today's youth are parents of the first generation that has grown up entirely in the new world that emerged between 1940 and 1960—the world of the bomb, the population explosion, the environmental crisis, and the planet-spanning communication grid.* Lightning-fast social changes have widened the communication and value gap between the generations to an unprecedented degree. This new world that has emerged has made many of the attitudes and ideas which we learned from past generations irrelevant to our children's future. This makes it a tough time to be an adolescent—or the parents of an adolescent. But it is also a potentially rewarding time.

To cope creatively with the future, Mead holds, there must be a new kind of communication and collaboration between those who are older and the young, who are most at home in the new world and most involved with that future. Enough trust must be developed between the generations to permit older adults, who have the essential skills and handles of power, to work with youth and young adults in finding workable answers to the crucial questions many youth and young adults are asking, questions such as "What will enable humanity to survive on a livable planet?" The challenge, to both adults and youth, is to pioneer in developing a new kind of collaboration between the generations so that we can search together for the answers to the problems threatening our planet's future!

Parenting Your Parents

One of the most difficult experiences of mid-years couples is the reversal of roles, as aging parents become increasingly dependent on them—emotionally if not physically. Seeing the once-competent parents we love waste away and lose their ability to handle and enjoy life is an agonizing experience for everyone involved.

Responding lovingly and appropriately to the needs and demands of aging parents can occur to the extent that we are able to keep our Adult side in control when we're with them. To do this usually requires completing unfinished growth work. In particular, it requires becoming a more nurturing Parent to our own inner Child, so that that side of us can relinquish the hope and need to have our parents always available as nurturers. The behavior of aging parents will not so easily activate our inner Child if our Adult side, and not our needy inner Child, is in the driver's seat. The death of parents will be less traumatic, though still very painful, if this growth work has been accomplished and the inner dependency on them relinquished to a considerable degree.

As the health of aging parents declines, an existential chill settles over the psyche of a mid-years person. But becoming a parent to one's parents provides an opportunity to express our love, assuage our guilt, and do anticipatory grief work preparing for their eventual death. The death of parents is a challenge and an opportunity to do unfinished growing up. Anger and fear wells up from the inner Child who feels deserted. This provides an opportunity to be a caring, nurturing Parent to one's inner Child. The death of parents also provides an opportunity for one's Adult to discover that it *can* cope with the new reality this brings, and use the new sense of inner freedom of which it may become aware.

Creative Possibilities of the Empty Nest

For several weeks after our last child left home, Charlotte and I experienced heaviness, antagonism, and emotional distancing. It took us a while (in spite of the fact that we are both counselors) to realize that *we* were in a grief reaction. For the first time in over twenty-five years, we were together in our home for an extended period without children. It was not until we expressed and began to resolve our conflicted feelings of loss and release that our depression lifted and we became aware of some of the new possibilities of our empty nest.

Given present life expectancies, the average couple will have approximately sixteen years together after the last child leaves—almost as long as they had together with children in the home. If a couple has done little to nurture their relationship through the years, the exodus of children usually reveals a painful marital vacuum. Many couples simply split at that point without discovering if they could revive and renew their relationship. Even couples who have not neglected their relationship may encounter stress as they struggle to relearn how to live alone without the children, creatively. Fortunately most couples make this transition and are happier together than during the child-rearing years. Studies reveal that after the children leave the nest there is a gradual rise in the degree of marital satisfaction.*

Parental concern and worry about children continue, and may even be intensified, after the children have left home. Parents wonder: Will they make it on their own? Will they succeed in developing fulfilling lives as adults? The struggles of young adult children with educational, vocational, and marital problems are particularly painful to parents because they realize that there is so little they can do to help. Accepting the fact that our children must make it on their own, and in their own way, is a difficult but necessary aspect of coping creatively with the empty nest.

Couples need to do three things to discover the creative possibilities of the empty nest. The first is to face, talk through, and resolve the big feelings, including the grief that accompanies any major change in one's life situation. If you're into the empty nest experience, or on the verge of it, I suggest that you each list in your growth log all your feelings about this new reality in your lives—the anxiety, grief, freedom, depression, anger, expectation, loss, remorse, emptiness, and joy. Then express to your partner the feelings you have listed and discuss them. Pour them out and talk them through. Take as much time as you need to resolve these feelings so that your awareness of the new possibilities and the open future can increase.

The second aspect of creative coping is to develop actively the new possibilities and fresh options that are open to you as a couple. Anne Simon puts the challenge well: "Sixteen new marriage years, more or less, can spark an intensity unsuspected when there were young children and youthful struggles absorbing time and energy. Who will settle for mediocre, end-of-the-road marriage when there is a chance for lively interchange?"*

List in your growth log all the things that you would like to do with your spouse, now that most parental responsibilities have diminished drastically. Compare your list with that of your spouse and make plans together to do those things which appeal to both of you. If there is little or no overlap between your lists, you probably need to participate in a marriage enrichment group. That could be helpful even if your lists are nearly identical.

The third aspect of creative coping is to invest some of the time and energy that the empty nest has now made available in developing and enjoying your own *individual* talents and interests. For a woman whose vocation has been mainly or exclusively homemaking, this may mean developing a new vocation, or reviving a long-dormant one, outside the home.

List in your growth log the things that you would like to do to develop your separate interests. Then discuss your list and your spouse's with each other, focusing on how you can balance your togetherness and apartness. In light of your discussion, make concrete plans to begin realizing one or more of your individual dreams. Discuss your plans with each other. If both persons develop some autonomous interests it helps prevent sticky overdependency on each other. This is an important preparation for the years of retirement and for the eventual challenge of widowhood or widowerhood. To cope with the empty nest creatively, couples need to make the happy discovery that "The empty nest is actually crowded with possibilities."*

An Empty Nest Enrichment Group

A mid-years minister in Southern California decided that his church could become a more effective people-development center by expanding its growth group program.† He sensed that one group which was needed was an empty nest marriage enrichment group. Five couples were recruited. The pastor and his wife served as cofacilitators as well as participants. The group's contract included these purposes: to enable couples to develop the freedom to grow and to become growth agents for each other; to understand the dynamics of the empty nest stage of marriage, both as a crisis period and as highly creative, productive years; to help couples increase their communication skills and their experiences of the many facets of intimacy; to increase the spiritual quality of their relationships including Christian values; to develop a network of support and trust among them and a sense of outreach to other couples.

The group agreed to have six weekly 2½-hour meetings, plus an all-day Saturday retreat. The sessions included these activities: "community building" experiences; active listening and trust exercises; couple communication work; input; and discussion periods. Each session concluded with experiential worship. The last session included a service of renewing marital covenants, planned by the group. In the post-series evaluation, participants expressed appreciation for the new communication tools they had learned, the growth they had experienced, and the warm support that had developed in the group.

This group illustrates some of the exciting possibilities for mutual support and enrichment. If such groups were available before and during the early part of the empty nest stage, more and more couples would discover the rich potentialities of Mid-Years II. They would experience the mutual help of a caring community as they remodel their marriage for maximum enjoyment and growth together.

Enriching Life by Facing Death

The empty nest stage is a time of increasingly frequent losses. To deal constructively with grief is essential to a good life during these years. After the recent funeral of a relative of our parents' generation, Charlotte said, "I was thinking during the service how many of these we'll be attending in the next few years."

A good way to cope with mid-years losses is to participate in a grief growth group. (The process of setting up and leading such a group has been described elsewhere.*) Every significant loss tends to stir up awareness of the eventual death of oneself and one's mate. Therefore, an important aspect of mid-years marital creativity is to deal with one's gut-level feelings about death. Doing this important growth work can enhance the sense of the preciousness of each day of one's life and marriage.

A minister in the Pacific Northwest has been leading what she calls "Living with Dying" groups to help people deal constructively with feelings about dying and death.† The groups meet for five weekly 2-hour sessions, using Elisabeth Kübler-Ross's *On Death and Dying* as a resource to be read between meetings.‡ The first hour of each session is spent discussing topics from the book. The group then divides into two subgroups, led by the minister and her co-facilitator, for experiential and feeling-level sharing, including debriefing on such between-session assignments as: "Talk to three people about death, being aware of how they respond" or "Imagine that you have only a limited time to live and try to say how this awareness influences your feelings about your lifestyle and present relationship."

Unfaced or unresolved anxieties about death—existential anxieties—are a significant dimension of many mid-years problems, including marriage problems. A grief growth group or a living-with-dying group can help mid-years persons do their growth work around these anxieties by providing the most favorable context—a caring community. If we face our anxieties in the context of an honest, growing faith and within relationships of trust, it is possible to transform at least some of the anxiety into motivation for living life more fully and creatively.

I recall an experience of hospitalization several years ago, when I was inundated by nameless anxieties quite out of proportion to the seriousness of my medical condition. My inner crisis gradually subsided as I began to confront my fears of dying. When I was released from the hospital, I had a remarkable experience. It was as though a veil had been removed from my eyes. The sky seemed bluer and the grass a more vivid green than I had seen it in years!

A Quaker writer speaks to the condition of many of us in the mid-years:

> No one has reached maturity until he has learned to face the fact of his own death and shape his life accordingly. Then the true perspective emerges. The preoccupation with . . . accumulating goods, or fame or power, is exposed. Then every morning seems fresh and new, as indeed it is. Each flower, each leaf, every greeting from a friend, every letter from a distance, every poem and every song strikes with double impact, as if we were sensing them for the first and for the last time. Once we accept the fact that we shall disappear, we also discover the larger self which relates us to our family and friends, to our neighborhood and community, to nation, humanity, and indeed, to the whole creation from which we have sprung. We are a part of all this, too, and death cannot entirely withdraw us from it. To the extent that we have poured ourselves into all of these . . . we live on in them. . . . So the divine spark kindled in us can never really be extinguished, for it is part of a universal flame.*

8. Growth Counseling for Mid-Years Marriage Crises

Each of us may perceive various differences, qualities, or behavior in the other as *undesirable*. . . . But we also grow through grappling with the impasse these differences may bring. Staying with it through the impasse, and growing through them requires courage, trust, honesty, and effort; yet it is here, only in the honest confrontation of self with another through *time* and *change* in the intimate and caring relationship, that the greatest depths of personal and emotional growth can occur.*

—Nena and George O'Neill

Many mid-years couples are in pain, including many who on the surface seem to have no major hang-ups. For some, there is a cauldron of disappointment, resentment, boredom, and emptiness beneath the facade they present to the outside world. Some have been in a quiet crisis of growing alienation for years. In some such cases divorce may be the only way out of a paralyzed and paralyzing relationship; it may offer the only chance for a more potentializing future for the two persons. But in other cases couples can rebuild their relationship on a more growth-producing contract, if they are willing to work hard with a skilled counselor.

Many mid-years couples in marital crisis have had a functional marriage down through the years. Their relationship has simply been thrown off keel by the heavy pressure of multiple losses, changing roles, and diminished self-esteem. They still have a lot invested in their marriage, which is one reason for the intensity of their fighting. Though deeply distressed, they still value many things about their relationship. With the help of a skilled pastoral counselor or marriage counselor, many such couples not only weather the storm but develop a stronger relationship as a result of learning to handle it. This chapter describes some of the approaches by which couples in mid-years crisis can be helped to grow through counseling.

Marriage Growth Counseling

The growth counseling approach is particularly useful in helping individuals and couples handle severe mid-years stresses constructively. I have described the philosophy and basic methods of marriage growth counseling elsewhere.* The approach seeks to help couples use crises as growth opportunities. It awakens hope by activating the couple's latent resources for taking action within their marriage to increase the satisfaction of mutual needs.

In counseling sessions two questions can help a counselor ascertain whether short-term marriage counseling, as contrasted to longer-term marriage therapy, is likely to be effective: "Have there been good periods in your marriage? If so, tell me about them." Later the counselor may ask: "In spite of your pain, what do you still like about your marriage (or your partner)?" The second question should be asked only after the anger and hurt have been drained off by thorough ventilation. If it is asked prematurely, the caring that may still be there in the relationship is buried beneath anger and hurt. If couples can recall good times in the past or become aware of what they each still like in the marriage, their hope may be awakened; the renewal of hope increases motivation to change. If two people have had no good periods together and have nothing that they still like in the marriage, the prognosis is poor. Short-term marriage crisis counseling will probably not suffice. However, the best way to discover if they really need long-term marriage therapy is to try short-term crisis counseling methods for several sessions.

Many mid-years couples feel deeply embarrassed and hopeless about themselves and their relationship by the time they come for counseling. It is important to affirm them and to introduce the growth perspective in the counseling by statements such as these: "It takes strength to recognize that you need help and then do something to get it." "I realize that you both feel very discouraged about your marriage right now, for very understandable reasons. You're going through a time of severe pressures. This crisis confronts you with the need to strengthen your marriage so that it will be more satisfying to you both." "You've been through a lot of ups and downs together. You seem to have some important things still going *for* your marriage. It's likely that you'll be able to rebuild some of the satisfying things you've lost from your marriage, if you're both willing to work at it." Whatever the counselor says, of course, must be genuine and appropriate to what he or she perceives in a particular relationship.

Resources for Mid-Years Counseling

Most of the guidelines and methods described in the first seven chapters of this book can be used in mid-years marriage counseling as well as in enrichment sessions. Much mid-years marriage counseling is simply personal instruction and coaching to help a couple apply the twelve strategies (chap. 2) in their individual lives and in their relationship to one another. Almost all mid-years couples who come for counseling need help in strengthening communication and in revising their priorities and values. Often dull sex, spiritual poverty, and crises with adolescents contribute to the escalating problems that brought them for help. In many cases, an unresolved bereavement coincided with the drastic worsening of their marital pain. For this reason, it is wise to ask all mid-years persons in counseling: "Have you had any major loss in the last few years?" If they have, and the grief wound is not yet healed, the first and perhaps the most basic help they need is in completing their grief work.*

Most mid-years couples in severe crises need to revise their marital contracts radically. Many such couples are hurting because of lopsided, unfair contracts. It is essential in counseling, therefore, to raise their consciousness and increase their awareness of the need to correct this injustice.

After a couple's anger and pain have diminished, and their

blocked communication channels are reopened, it is helpful to introduce them to the Intentional Marriage Method as modified for use in counseling.* This is a hope-awakening tool which can give a couple the satisfaction of succeeding in revising one part of their contract at a time. After they have discovered that they *can* improve their working agreement, they should be coached in systematic revision of all aspects of the contract which are unfair to one person or are areas of chronic conflict (chap. 3). Because of the severe communication blocks present in most couples who come for counseling, it is helpful to have them write out their understanding of their contract, including the revisions.

As a couple takes each small step in implementing more mutually growth-producing ways of relating, the counselor should encourage them by expressing appreciation of their progress. This affirmation helps a couple keep on struggling to learn new communication and conflict-resolution skills, until their use of these tools produces enough satisfactions to make the process self-reinforcing and therefore self-perpetuating.

Transactional Analysis is useful to many mid-years couples in crisis counseling. Many couples have been playing destructive Parent-Child games for years, each trying vainly to make the other an always-nurturing Parent or an always-submissive Child figure. Most of the futile, destructive conflicts and many of the sexual problems stem directly from this circular Parent-Child interaction. I recall several instances in which the underlying cause of a husband's or a wife's affair was that person's Child side striking out rebelliously at the controlling Parent in the other. Parent-Child games reach a point of diminishing returns for many in mid-life. "Games," in T.A.'s understanding, are forms of repetitive, mutual manipulation which are substitutes for intimacy. If one partner —usually the wife—experiences consciousness raising and stops playing one side of a long-standing Parent-Child game, chaos usually erupts. This kind of pain is a sign of hope, since it indicates that at least one person is fed up and may be open to developing a more mutually satisfying, Adult-to-Adult relationship.

I have described ways of using T.A. in resolving marital conflict elsewhere.* Suffice it here to say that if both persons respond to the counselor's initial presentation of the P-A-C concepts, they should then be coached in using this tool to interrupt Parent-Child transactions and in learning to relate on an Adult-to-Adult basis. It is also important for them to identify and interrupt the one or two favorite games which have dominated their interaction for years. As Eric Berne pointed out, the all-time favorite marriage game is "If it weren't for you. . . ." It isn't easy to relinquish games that have been practiced throughout a marriage. But if the "pay-offs" of a game are no longer satisfying, many couples can do it, once they become aware of their games and the painful price of playing them. I often say to a couple: "You may not be able to turn off the old Parent-Child tape recordings fully, but your Adult can decide whether or not to be controlled by their messages." Individuals exercise their Adult sides by deciding and acting constructively. As they do, their Adult grows stronger and more able to guide their lives and their relationships.

If There Has Been an Affair

Frequently the crisis that brings a couple to counseling is the discovery by one partner that the other has had an affair. It is important to help couples understand the underlying causes of an affair. It is useful to distinguish between situational infidelity and chronic, repetitive patterns of infidelity. The latter often are driven by compulsive craving for reassurance about one's masculinity or femininity, or by a vain attempt to fill the emptiness of not having had a satisfying relationship in childhood with the parent of the other sex. In such cases, the prognosis for any treatment except long-term individual and marital therapy is not hopeful.

In most other affairs, the fundamental cause is chronic neglect of each other and of the marriage, and the consequent accumulation of hurt, anger, resentment, and alienation. The affair is then a symptom of a barren relationship and of the mutual need deprivation that has produced this condition. It is essential to help the "offended" partner see how he or she contributed significantly to the malnourished relationship that made it easy for the affair to occur. A husband, for example, who is "married to his job" and spends little time with his wife, is inviting marital trouble.

Affairs in the mid-years often are "last flings." They are desperate attempts to recapture one's lost youth or find moments of ecstasy to offset a dull, dreary marriage "before it's too late." Such affairs often are unconscious attempts to quiet one's fear of aging and death by relating intimately with a younger person.

In counseling, the offended partner should be encouraged to postpone drastic steps, such as initiating divorce proceedings, until he or she has dealt with feelings of intense anger and hurt. Doing this makes possible a more rational decision. In many cases, mid-years couples discover that they are better off staying with their long-term marriage than dissolving the relationship in hopes of finding greener pastures elsewhere. Affairs often are short-lived, partly because they fail to realize the dream of eternal youth for which the person is searching. If both marriage partners are willing to work together in counseling to rebuild their relationship on a new and stronger foundation, they may be able to use their painful crisis as an opportunity to grow together.

Constructive Divorce and New Beginnings

Mid-years realism and heightened awareness of swiftly passing time can help some persons face the fact that their only hope for a fulfilling life is to end a dead or deadening marriage. Speaking of their middle-aged friends whose marriages break up, Bernice and Morton Hunt observe: "While middle age can be a lengthy, joyous, liberated, fulfilling, and intensely pleasurable period of life, it is not likely to be any of those (except lengthy) if spent in the imprisonment of an outworn, outgrown, and loveless marriage. Divorce can be the greatest liberation of all for those who really need it."* For couples who married for deeply neurotic reasons, or where one has grown and the other has not—or both have grown in different directions—or where one has no interest in developing a more growth-producing marriage, divorce may be an essential step toward growth.

The growth counselor's function is to help such persons as they work through their resistance to bury a dead relationship; uncouple without infighting so as to avoid further hurt to each other and to their children; agree on a plan for the children that will be best for the children's mental health; work through the ambivalent feelings that usually accompany divorce—guilt, rage, release, resentment, failure, joy, loss—so that each person's infected grief wound can heal; discover what each contributed to the disintegration of their relationship; learn the relationship-building and love-nurturing skills which each will need either to enjoy creative singlehood or to establish a better marriage. Divorce counseling should help each individual move through the pain, utilizing the growth opportunity in the pain to prepare for a new and better chapter in life.

A person's divorce growth work can be facilitated best by a combination of individual growth counseling and a divorce growth group.† A divorce growth group is a support and mutual-help group, similar to a grief group, in which divorcing persons share and work through their feelings and help each other make sound decisions in coping with the host of problems that single and divorced people face in a couple society. With over a million divorces in the nation each year, society desperately needs a network of such small growth groups in which persons can experience a caring community. A divorce growth group is an essential part of a church's mid-years enrichment program. Through such a group, a mutual ministry of caring and growth can be implemented. As a participant in one such group declared: "I've discovered, in this group, that what I thought was the end, is really a new beginning!"

An Invitation: The Challenge of Mid-Years Pioneering

Interest in exploring human consciousness and developing human potentials is flourishing today in our society like flowers in a spring meadow. There is a proliferation of human growth centers—many of them church related—and an expanding interest in methods of enhancing consciousness, parapsychology, biofeedback, transpersonal psychology, and meditation. Duane S. Elgin, social policy analyst at Stanford University's Research Institute, holds that this surge of interest is neither a passing fad nor escapism from society's massive ills. Rather, it is an indication that an exciting new frontier has opened—that of "realizing our collective potential" by exploring and developing inner space. Speaking of human consciousness, Elgin declares, "Metaphorically, it is as though we live and love in a small, cramped, one-room house—thinking that this room is our home in its entirety. Yet, if we were only to become aware, we would find that our house is a mansion of many different rooms."*

The new frontier of consciousness and relationships offer both new opportunities and new resources to those who find excitement in spiritual pioneering. Churches and their leaders—both ministers and laity—have a major stake in the full exploration of the frontier of spiritual growth. They have significant contributions to make to the development of this exciting new terrain.

Pioneering on the new frontier is a natural for mid-years persons. Many persons in the mid-years bring unique resources to this adventure: the realism and mature perspective which come from long experience; the blend of toughness and tenderness derived from coping with pain and problems; the awareness of the need to revivify one's own faith and guiding values; the conviction that the quality of one's relationships—with self, others, nature, and God—is, in the final analysis, what matters most.

Success in developing this rapidly opening frontier of humankind's collective potential may well provide a key to survival on a livable planet. We will be liberated from our obsession with things only if we devote ourselves to the growth of persons in and through their relationships. Pioneering on the human development frontier, as Elgin points out, requires commitment to two interdependent ethical principles—an *ecological ethic* which motivates us to treat the whole earth with care and respect, and a *human wholeness ethic* which enables us to major in the growth of persons.* As we nurture human growth, we must simultaneously befriend the total environment, so that the fullest development of persons will be possible into the far distant future.

The growth-ecology frontier is open and inviting. Best of all, pioneering on this frontier begins where you are—with your own inner growth, with the growth of your close relationships, with the growth of your friendship with nature and the Spirit, and with your efforts to change the institutions of which you are a part so that they will be environments which stimulate and support the growth of persons. The frontier is open! Welcome to the adventure that awaits you!

Notes

Page
iv. * Gardner, *Self-Renewal*, p. xv.
iv. † C. Clinebell, *Meet Me in the Middle*, p. 50.
1.   * Simon, *The New Years*, pp. 282–83.
1.   † Studies by Bernice Neugarten of the University of Chicago show that both middle-class men and women tend to see middle age as a time of rewards and prime activity, whereas working-class men and women tend to see these as years of decline. *Science Digest*, October 1958, p. 21.
6.   * Roger Gould, "Adult Life Stages: Growth toward Self-Tolerance," *Psychology Today*, February 1975, p. 74.
7.   * LeShan, *Crisis of Middle Age*, p. 236.
7.   † Erik Erikson, *Gandhi's Truth* (New York: Norton, 1969), p. 395.
9.   * Alvin R. Voelkner, "Challenge for Church: A Middle-Aged Majority," *Our Sunday Visitor*, 23 February 1975, p. 10.
10. * LeShan, p. 2.
11. * Hunt and Hunt, *Prime Time*, p. 20.
12. * LeShan, p. 265.
16. * Herman Feifel reports these studies; cited in Margaretta K. Bowers et al., *Counseling the Dying* (New York: Nelson and Sons, 1964), p. 2.
16. † O'Neill and O'Neill, *Shifting Gears*, p. 74.
19. * Transactional Analysis is a system which is remarkably useful in understanding and improving interpersonal relationships. If you're not familiar with the T.A. concept of the inner Parent, Adult, and Child, see Eric Berne, *Games People Play* (New York: Grove Press, 1964), chapter 1 for a succinct overview. When Parent, Adult, and Child—and Adolescent—are capitalized in this book, they refer to these four parts *within* a person.
21. * Abraham Maslow, *Motivation and Personality* (New York: Harper & Row, 1954), p. 239.
22. * This image is from *The Spouse Gap*, by Lee and Casebier.
22. † August Gribbins, "An American Fantasy: Scoring in the Mating Game," *Los Angeles Times*, 30 November 1975.
22. ‡ Peterson, *Married Love in the Middle Years*, p. 54; and Judith Long Laws, "A Feminist View of Marital Adjustment," in Gurman and Rice, *Couples in Conflict*, pp. 92–93.
23. * Gould, "Adult Life Stages," pp. 76–77.
23. † For a fuller discussion of positive fidelity and equality in marriages, see H. Clinebell, *Growth Counseling for Marriage Enrichment*, pp. 23–25.
24. * Ibid., "Relationship-Building Tools," pp. 28–36, and "Enrichment Retreats and Groups," pp. 37–47. See also H. Clinebell, *The People Dynamic*, chaps. 2, 3, and 4.
26. * Clinebell and Clinebell, *The Intimate Marriage*, pp. 37–39, gives the forms and instructions for their use.
26. † William Lederer and Don Jackson, "How to Check Up Your Own Marriage," in *The Mirages of Marriage* (New York: W. W. Norton, 1968), chap. 50, pp. 363–71.
29. * The IMM is described in detail in H. Clinebell, *Growth Counseling for Marriage Enrichment*, chap. 2, pp. 10–17.
29. † Ibid. For methods of recruiting see p. 46.
30. * Ibid., pp. 74–76.
31. * Martin Buber, *At the Turning* (New York: Farrar, Strauss and Young, 1952), p. 44.
32. * Gould, p. 76. The majority of respondents under 35 answered "agree" to the statement, "There's still plenty of time to do most of the things I want

to do." From ages 34 to 41 an increasing percentage disagreed. After 55, the proportion of "agrees" declined steadily.

32. † Ibid., p. 74.
32. ‡ See Viktor Frankl, *The Doctor and the Law, An Introduction to Logotherapy* (New York: Alfred A. Knopf, 1962).
36. * *Time*, 29 July 1966, p. 54.
37. * The writer of these words was Sandra Albertson; used by permission.
38. * See Abraham H. Maslow, *Religions, Values, and Peak Experiences* (Columbus: Ohio State University Press, 1964), pp. 91–96.
38. † Lecture at Claremont, Calif., 20 June 1970.
39. * Richard Evans, *Dialogue with Erik Erikson* (New York: Harper & Row, 1967), p. 51.
40. * Carl Gustav Jung, *Modern Man in Search of a Soul* (London: Routledge and Kegan Paul, 1943), p. 264.
40. † Gardner, *Self-Renewal.*
41. * Clinebell and Clinebell, *The Intimate Marriage*, p. 179.
42. * See Simon, "The Vintage Mind," chap. 8.
42. † This is a paraphrase of a statement attributed to Robert M. Hutchins.
42. ‡ Robert Butler, "The Destiny of Creativity in Later Life," in *Psychodynamic Studies on Aging: Creativity, Reminiscing and Dying,* ed. Sidney Levin and Ralph J. Kahana (New York: International Universities Press, 1967), pp. 50–51.
43. * From a personal communication.
43. † See Benson, *The Relaxation Response.*
43. ‡ Lewis and Streitfeld, *Growth Games,* p. 57. For a helpful section on meditation, see pp. 57–74.
46. * For further methods of liberation see the two books by Charlotte H. Clinebell listed in the Annotated Bibliography.
46. †Abraham Maslow, "Self-Actualization and Beyond," in James F. T. Bugental, *Challenges of Humanistic Psychology* (New York: McGraw-Hill, 1967), p. 283.
46. ‡ Abraham Maslow, *Toward a Psychology of Being,* 2d ed. (New York: D. van Nostrand, 1968), p. 210.
47. * See Lewis and Streitfeld, pp. 72–75.
47. † Fritz Kunkel, *Creation Continues* (Waco, Texas: Word, 1973), pp. 267–77.
49. * The term *basic trust* is from Erik Erikson, *Childhood and Society* (New York: W. W. Norton, 1950).
49. † This is the way Paul Tillich described the experience of grace.
49. ‡ Martin Buber, *I and Thou,* trans. Ronald Gregor Smith, 2d ed. (New York: Scribner's Sons, 1958), p. 75.
50. * "Sexuality of Older People Can Be Better," *Toronto Globe and Mail,* 21 October 1971.
50. † Alex Comfort, ed., *The Joy of Sex* (New York: Crown, 1972), p. 220.
50. ‡ William H. Masters and Virginia E. Johnson, *The Human Sexual Response* (Boston: Little, Brown & Co., 1966). The following statements by the authors, sex researchers, summarize their findings on this issue: "There is no time limit drawn by the advancing years to female sexuality" (p. 247). "If elevated levels of sexual activity are maintained . . . and if neither acute nor chronic physical incapacity intervenes, aging males usually are able to continue some form of active sexual expression into the 70 and 80 age group" (p. 263).
50. § Morton Hunt, "Sexual Behavior in the 1970s," *Playboy,* October, 1973, p. 88. The scientific survey was conducted by The Research Guild, Inc.
51. * Ibid.
51. † This statement and the description of the myths are by Robert M. Butler, as reported by Al Rossiter, Jr., "Aging and Sexuality Not Incompatible," *St. Paul Pioneer Press,* 7 April 1974, p. W3.
53. * William H. Masters and Virginia Johnson, *The Pleasure Bond: A New Look at Sexuality and Commitment* (Boston: Little, Brown & Co., 1974), pp. 107–8.
53. † Ibid., chap. 4. See also C. Clinebell, "Liberated Sex," in *Meet Me in the Middle,* chap. 5.
53. ‡ H. Clinebell, *Growth Counseling for Marriage Enrichment,* chap. 2.
54. * Masters and Johnson, p. 268.
54. † Butler, as reported in Rossiter, p. W3.
54. ‡ See above note, p. 19.
57. * Gribbins, "An American Fantasy," p. 7.
59. * Charles L. Morgan, as quoted in McCary, *Freedom and Growth in Marriage,* p. 97.

60. * Before using this communication tool, I suggest that you read H. Clinebell, *Growth Counseling for Marriage Enrichment,* chap. 2.
61. * Ann Steinmann and David Fox, *The Male Dilemma: How to Survive the Sexual Revolution* (New York: Jason Aronson, 1975), p. 174.
61. † Information about well-trained marriage and family counselors can be obtained by writing The American Association of Marriage and Family Counselors, 225 Yale Ave., Claremont, CA 91711, or The American Association of Pastoral Counselors, 3 West 29th St., New York, NY 10001.
62. * Write ACME, 495 South Church St., P.O. Box 10596, Winston-Salem, NC 27108.
62. † See Annotated Bibliography.
62. ‡ See Thomas Gordon, *Parent Effectiveness Training* (New York: Peter H. Wyden, 1970).
62. § Cassette course IIIB, "Enriching Parent-Child Relationships," in H. Clinebell, *Growth Counseling,* Part I, describes such an event and suggests other ways of enhancing parent-teen relating, including a healthy family growth interview.
62. ‖ For information on "family clusters" write Dr. Margaret Sawin, Box 8452, 12 Corners Branch, Rochester, NY 14618.
63. * See above note p. 19.
64. * Margaret Mead, *Culture and Commitment: A Study of the Generation Gap,* (Garden City, New York: Doubleday, 1970).
66. * For a report on the research findings, see Laws, "A Feminist View of Marital Adjustment," pp. 92–93.
67. * Simon, p. 283.
68. * LeShan, p. 240.
68. † Edwin C. Linberg, Temple City Christian Church (Disciples of Christ), Temple City, Calif.
69. * See cassette course 2B, "A Grief Recovery Group"; and 2A, "Helping and Being Helped by the Dying," in H. Clinebell, *Growth Counseling:* Part II—*Coping Constructively with Crises.* See also Oates, *Pastoral Counseling in Grief and Separation.*
69. † Jane A. Raible, Everett Unitarian Fellowship, Everett, Wash.
69. ‡ Elizabeth Kübler-Ross, *On Death and Dying* (New York: Macmillan, 1969).
70. * Bradford Smith, "Dear Gift of Life," *Pendle Hill Pamphlet No. 142* Wallingford, Pa. (1965).
71. * O'Neill and O'Neill, pp. 216–17.
72. * See H. Clinebell, "Helping Couples in Crisis," in *Marriage Enrichment,* chap. 8.
73. * For methods of helping persons do their grief work, see Oates, *Grief and Separation*; also H. Clinebell's cassette course 2B, "A Grief Recovery Group."
74. * See above note, p. 72.
75. * H. Clinebell, *Basic Types of Pastoral Counseling* (Nashville: Abingdon, 1966), pp. 134–36. For a "live" illustration of the use of T.A. in a growth counseling session, listen to cassette course 3A, "Using Marriage Problems for Growth," in *Growth Counseling: Enriching Marriage and Family Life.*
77. * Hunt and Hunt, pp. 61–62.
77. † The cassette course 3B, "The Crisis of Divorce—Growth Opportunities," in H. Clinebell, *Growth Counseling* includes segments of a divorce group, with a discussion of the principles of setting up such a group.
78. * Duane S. Elgin, "What Waits Beyond America's Newest Frontier?", *Los Angeles Times,* 19 December 1974.
79. * Ibid.

Annotated Bibliography

Benson, Herbert. *The Relaxation Response*. New York: William Morrow, 1975. A simple approach to meditation; relates various forms of meditation to physical illness and health.

Clinebell, Charlotte H. *Counseling for Liberation*. Philadelphia: Fortress, 1976. Methods of relating counseling and consciousness raising.

————. *Meet Me in the Middle: On Becoming Human Together*. New York: Harper and Row, 1973. A guide to changing roles and liberation in marriage, sex, and child rearing.

Clinebell, Howard J., Jr. *Growth Counseling*. Nashville: Abingdon, 1973, 1974. Fifteen cassette training courses with *User's Guide*. Part I— *Enriching Marriage and Family Life* includes courses on leading enrichment groups, enhancing sex, and parent-child relationships. Part II—*Coping Constructively With Crises* includes courses on the crises of the mid-years, grief, divorce, and adolescence.

————. *Growth Counseling for Marriage Enrichment, Pre-Marriage and the Early Years*. Philadelphia: Fortress, 1975. The basic principles and methods of growth counseling and marriage enrichment, with particular attention to preparation for marriage and early marriage enrichment.

————. *The People Dynamic: Changing Self and Society Through Growth Groups*. New York: Harper and Row, 1972. Principles and methods of leading growth groups— marriage, youth, and parent-child groups.

Clinebell, Howard J., Jr., and Clinebell, Charlotte H. *Crisis and Growth: Helping Your Troubled Child*. Philadelphia:

Fortress, 1971. A guide for helping children cope with crises.

————. *The Intimate Marriage.* New York: Harper and Row, 1970. A guide for use by couples and in marriage enrichment groups. Should be used in conjunction with *Meet Me in The Middle.*

Comfort, Alex, ed. *More Joy: A Companion to the Joy of Sex.* New York: Crown, 1974. A resource for developing playful sex.

Gardner, John W. *Self-Renewal, The Individual and the Innovative Society.* New York: Harper and Row, 1964. A challenge to renew integrity, purpose, and commitment in the complexities of modern life.

Gurman, Alan S. and Rice, David G., eds. *Couples in Conflict.* New York: Jason Aronson, 1975. New directions and methods in marital therapy.

Hall, Bryan P. *Value Clarification as Learning Process: A Guidebook.* New York: Paulist, 1973. Principles, exercises, and classroom and conference strategies for redefining values.

Howe, Reuel L. *The Creative Years.* Greenwich, Conn.: Seabury, 1959. Creativity in middle-years marriage, work, sex, faith, and parenthood.

Hunt, Bernice, and Hunt, Morton. *Prime Time: A Guide to the Pleasures and Opportunities of the New Middle Age.* New York: Stein and Day, 1975. A personal, practical discussion of the new possibilities of the mid-years.

Irwin, Paul B. *The Care and Counseling of Youth in the Church.* Philadelphia: Fortress, 1975. A guide to a creative ministry to youth.

Johnson, Paul E. *The Middle Years.* Philadelphia: Fortress, 1971. A resource for loaning to mid-years counselees.

Kaplan, Helen Singer. *The Illustrated Manual of Sex Therapy.* New York: Quadrangle, 1975. A guide to sex therapy including the use of sensate focus techniques.

Lee, Robert, and Casebier, Marjorie. *The Spouse Gap: Weathering the Marriage Crisis During Middlescence.* Nashville: Abingdon, 1971. An analysis of the mid-years marriage crisis.

LeShan, Eda J. *The Wonderful Crisis of Middle Age.* New York: David McKay, 1973. Personal reflections and suggestions for self-actualization in the mid-years.

Lewis, H. R., and Streitfeld, H. S. *Growth Games.* New York: Harcourt, Jovanovich, 1970. Communication exercises for expanding consciousness, enlivening one's body, and building relationships.

McCary, James L. *Freedom and Growth in Marriage.* Santa Barbara: Wiley-Hamilton, 1975. An illustrated, topical resource book on growth-centered marriage.

Neugarten, Bernice L., ed. *Middle Age and Aging.* Chicago: University of Chicago Press, 1968. A reader in social psychology.

Neugarten, Bernice L., and Berkowitz, Howard. *Personality in Middle and Late Life.* New York: Atherton, 1964. Research findings on these life stages.

Oates, Wayne E. *Pastoral Counseling in Grief and Separation.* Philadelphia: Fortress, 1975. Discusses principles and methods which can be helpful to those facing the losses of the mid-years.

O'Neill, Nena, and O'Neill, George. *Shifting Gears: Finding Security in a Changing World.* New York: Avon, 1974. Guidelines for purposeful change and creative maturity.

Otto, Herbert A., ed. *Marriage and Family Enrichment: New Perspectives and Programs.* Nashville: Abingdon, 1976. Descriptions of marriage and family enrichment program and resources by twenty-one individuals or teams with experience in the field.

Pennington, Chester, and Pennington, Marjorie. *After the Children Leave Home.* Nashville: Graded, 1972. Coping constructively with the empty nest.

Peterson, James A. *Married Love in the Middle Years.* New York: Association, 1968. How to respond to the mid-years marital crisis.

Satir, Virginia. *Peoplemaking.* Palo Alto: Science and Be-

havior Books, 1972. A growth-oriented approach to parenting.

Simon, Anne W. *The New Years: A New Middle Age.* New York: Alfred P. Knopf, 1968. A challenge to pioneer in this new life stage.

Simons, Sidney B.; Howe, Leland W.; and Kirschenbaum, Howard. *Values Clarification: A Handbook of Practical Strategies for Teachers and Students.* New York: Hart Publishing Co., 1972. Seventy-nine practical techniques for clarifying and reformulating one's values.

Stone, Howard. *Crisis Counseling.* Philadelphia: Fortress Press, 1975. Principles of helping people handle crises constructively.

Tengbom, Mildred. *The Bonus Years.* Minneapolis: Augsburg, 1975. A religiously oriented approach to mid-years marriage, children, aging parents, and values.